MW01032127

GROWING A MORE HUMAN COMMUNITY

- VOLUME 1 -

CHILD

GROWING ME
Becoming a Child

by
Jim Wilder

Revised and updated 2024
from
The Complete Guide to Living With Men

Growing a More Human Community Volume I
Growing Me: *Becoming a Child*
Copyright© Jim Wilder 1993, 1997, 2004, 2024 All rights reserved.

Fast Track Press, Evergreen, CO 2024
ISBN 9798338219553
See LifeModelWorks.org for more on the Life Model.

Cover design by Sevag Shanlian

Growing a More Human Community

Volume I
CHILD
Growing Me: Becoming a Child

Volume II
ADULT
Growing Us: Becoming an Adult

Volume III
SENIOR
Growing We the People

Revised 2024
from
The Complete Guide to Living With Men
Copyright 1993, 1997, 2004
A Life Model book

Me was here!

I'm still finding "Me"

As-if-me is blocking me.

I don't really like part of the me.

Is there a path to find my me?

I lack the time and energy for half

the things Me wants to be.

Me may have found a topo map!

Table of Contents

About the author

I am now an old man who has lived a life that my grandchildren and their friends can neither imagine nor will ever see. I have been shaped by seventy years of observations in a variety of communities – some that no longer exist – and cultures that no longer function as they once did. My young friends cannot even imagine the relationships, patterns and options that had been a natural part of life for centuries or even millennia.

Life was neither easy nor ideal. Severe disabilities could be seen everywhere and considered part of life. The local priest believed I hid my hooves in my shoes (like devils of all other religions). I knew people who were convinced that going out under a full moon without a hat would drive them crazy.

We lived in a community where most people knew each other's grandparents and had opinions about what kind of people they were. Everyone could see how the lives of previous generations impacted their children and grandchildren. How we would grow up and get old seemed obvious to everyone. Our futures were illustrated by the families and generations around us. It seemed reasonable that our grandchildren would live among people who would remember what it was like living with us.

A stable community, one with memories of past generations, could be both secure and oppressive at times. Some people tended to remember the best about us while others permanently remembered our flaws – every mistake, failure and departure from the norms. While some seniors helped us learn and practice maturity, others blocked participation by younger people to enhance their own control and security. Some older people pushed us to perform and others never let the next generation participate.

It was obvious that some patterns did not turn out well and should be avoided. For example, conformity based on fears was tyrannical and produced civil unrest. One moment it was the conservative militia killing my neighbors, the next moment it was the Marxist rebels. Everyone carried the scars.

Staying with Paez Indian families in their traditional homes with traditional foods inspired my first fascination with other cultures. I was about eight and had been exposed to a number of cultures already but never noticed anything more than different languages and food.

Cultures became a life-long interest. One moment I would be eating hot dogs at Billy Graham's house and another I'd be camping with children from the Chicago housing projects. At Jeju (honeymoon island in Korea) I'd help an international gathering resolve tensions and on the Red Lake Indian Reservation work construction. I'd listen to children in South-central LA tell their stories about riots and travel through the Himalayas learning local stories and legends from my guides. Everywhere the cultures, stories and patterns held unique variations. But I am getting ahead of myself.

By the time I finished high school I was living in the USA. After a year of Bible school I attended Bemidji State and earned a BA in psychology and religious studies. I noticed that, while spiritual dimensions differed greatly, the major religions often agreed about how to treat one's own people and neighbors. My MA in theology and PhD in psychology came from Fuller Seminary.

Providing therapy in the Los Angeles area allowed me to know many people deeply. Quite a few had come from other places and cultures. Most of my professional work involved cleaning up after wars, abuse and neglect by people who had little idea what they might have done better.

Traveling as a teacher and speaker added a wealth of additional cultural dimensions. In Sri Lanka I met people recovering from a twenty-five year civil war. I watched Tamil and Sinhala people gather and learn to see each other through the eyes of heaven. Elephants rode to work on trucks and the deer at the tea plantation barked like dogs. I also learned what happens if you swallow one of the local peppers.

My cultural exploration continued expanding as I visited Chile, Germany, Poland, Hungary, Turkiye, Kenya, France, Thailand, Romania and other lands. In India I fought the mosquitoes, drank very sweet tea. Robert, a young man whose mother knew herbal remedies, provided a tasting tour of every health-improving tree and shrub. In Mexico, indigenous people from Chiapas comforted me when my mother died. South Sea Islanders took me into the Pacific Ocean where we stood eating what they found there. Speaking at international conferences and virtual meetings provided limited glimpses of many additional cultures such as China and Mongolia.

Being born during "la violencia" in Colombia, where approximately a quarter of a million people were killed by their neighbors, planted a desire in me to see people in communities become more human with one another. Kitty, my wife, grew up in Nigeria and lived through the

Biafran war. Her stories increased my awareness of the impact of war on children.

In the Killing Fields of Cambodia, Auschwitz, Birkenau and the ravine at Babi Yar Kiev I was reminded of walking through a pasture as a child and picking up a human skull laying among the bones on the ground. Decades of helping survivors, their children and grandchildren from the Russian Pogrom, Rwandan genocide, Armenian and Jewish Holocausts and government torture showed me the long shadow left by violence.

Many wars involved a religious conflict. Knowing the wars between Christian groups, I began teaching groups with divergent theologies how to live more relational lives. Raising joy and improving relational skills was my aim. I worked with Catholic, Ukrainian and Armenian Orthodox, Coptic, Anglican, Lutheran, Dutch Reformed, Presbyterian, Salvation Army, Messianic, Pentecostal, Baptist, Wesleyan and Anabaptist groups like Brethren, Mennonites and Amish.

My friendship with Fr. Ubald, who survived Rwandan genocides as both a child and again as an adult, developed from consulting on his documentary. A different documentary about the effects war on Armenian children opened conversations with my Armenian neighbors who had escaped with their lives.

Working with veterans in two VA hospitals helped me know the impact of war on adults and their families. Providing trauma recovery in South Sudan during their civil war and Ukraine during the Russian invasion revealed the impact of war violence on communities.

Perhaps because of these grim realities, I love outdoor adventures. In California the fun came from backpacking (a week at a time) in the high Sierra backcountry, climbing Mt. Whitney, meeting bears, finding a plane crash site and cross country skiing in the winter. In Europe I loved the Alps and the beautiful Carpathian mountains even when my local hosts insisted on visiting Count Dracula's castle. In South America I enjoyed visiting the indigenous villages in the Ecuadorian Andes and joining Colombian herdsmen chasing a jaguar in the Colombian mountains. In Brazil, the pygmy marmoset monkeys ran across the banana leaves to my delight.

In Northern Minnesota I enjoyed shooting white water rapids in a canoe when it was warm. For several summers I was a fishing guide and other summers I worked as a lifeguard at two state parks. Cross country skiing over frozen lakes made the best of the long winter. One morning the thermometer read -52F and I tossed a glass of water in the air outside to see if it would freeze before it hit the ground.

Fishing for halibut off the coast of Alaska or spearfishing off the California coast added other adventures. I was certified as a scuba diver with experience in night diving and deep diving. Eating scallops at depth was my favorite treat. By taking a zip-lock baggie of dipping sauce and harvesting scallops directly off the rocks I could eat them under water.

Camping around the USA on family trips year after year provided many views of nature. Watching fish, sea lions, dolphins or the sea turtles in Hawaii without bothering them was great fun. Underwater photography became another interest. Traveling and camping north of the arctic circle in Norway and the Lofoten Islands brought herds of reindeer, moose, sea otters and maybe a few trolls. Costa Rica's nature was diverse and beautiful. At the family wedding in Jamaica the local reggae bands motivated the wild life. I also enjoyed visiting windmills and tulips of the Netherlands, driving down the Rhine valley tasting the new wine and visiting castles with Kitty, my wife of almost fifty years. Visiting volcanoes, feeling big earthquakes and avoiding a small tsunami provided additional adventures.

I also like life at home. I built my own desk out of boards, fixed cars and, when we were poor students, I sewed dresses from McCalls's patterns for Kitty in exchange for her typing my papers. When we lived at a lower elevation I planted fruit trees and gardens. Baking casseroles (known in Minnesota as hot dishes), cookies and carrot cake was nice in cold weather. Cooking and improvising meals feels creative but I hate washing dishes.

I remodeled several of our homes. Most recently I moved a few walls and added some doors to create a walk-in closet. I added a balustrade to the stairway, replaced the wrap-around deck and added an automatic backup generator to the house.

Here in the Rocky Mountains, my spiritual daughter burns wood for heating. I like to fire up my chainsaw and down dead trees in the forest near her house for firewood. I sometimes bring over a little food, play my guitar and watch the fire in her wood stove.

I learned to play music in church. This led to playing in several bands, touring for a summer and being a studio guitarist for one record album. Most recently I played percussion in a worship band at church. Most evenings include some time making music which is even more fun when people stop by to play and sing along.

My creative expression began with my first microscope. Photomicrography led to learning photo processing in a darkroom. I did photography for college magazines and that eventually led to taking nature and underwater photographs. Television drew my interest and I became a TV cameraman for hockey games, concerts, lectures and eventually produced a number of instructional videos.

I enjoy machines. Technical interests like reading EEGs and PET scans provide practical help with my work in neurotheology. Learning to run printing presses, build computers, design and build circuit boards for research equipment and security systems have all been interests. I wrote code in binary, hexadecimal, machine language, Basic and Fortran. At one point I co-wrote a medical billing and accounting program in C++.

My main creative outlet has been in writing over twenty published books. The one book proposed by a publisher that I wrote for the market proved to be so frustrating that I didn't write again for five years. I also hate professional writing with all those citations to prove I am right. I like writing about topics that make sense to me and letting readers see if it makes sense to them. Sometimes, as I am writing, thoughts come to me that seem so interesting I have to stop and think about them for a while. Perhaps some of those thoughts reflect moments when my thinking is in touch with a greater mind than my own.

Preface to the 2024 Edition

When I was forty-nine I took a year off my work as a psychologist and minister to dream and write this book. The original title, Living with Men grew out of my observation that men produced a disproportionate amount of the relational damage and low joy I observed around me. Much of my professional work involved cleaning up from wars, abuse and negligent damage done by immature men who had little idea what they might have done better. Perhaps something could be learned from these observations.

While both men and women contribute to a stable, high-joy multigenerational community, men need a little more redemption. I intentionally focused on developing life-giving men. How does a community grow mature men who are good news for women, babies and the community itself?

In the twenty three years since the first version of this book was written much has changed. Many of the things that we once knew about growing up human have already been forgotten. Knowing how our lives impact our grandchildren slipped into oblivion. Patterns that once made sense no longer have a context. In this 2024 revision, I will say more about the context of community life. What might be important if we want to grow a stable multi-generational community? What would we want to avoid from past lessons learned?

I changed the title this book to *Growing a More Human Community*. This revision is divided into three books that address: 1) Becoming a child and growing an individual identity. 2) Becoming an adult and growing a group identity. 3) Becoming a senior and growing a sense of being one people across generations, genders and other differences.

Maturity seemed fairly obvious to people in the remote villages of the Andes mountains where I grew up. We had no car so we walked to most places. Rarely were we out of sight of someone who knew us. Travel in the mountains was usually on horses. No phones, computers, internet or even television were to be found. Human interactions were a constant activity and maturity was measured by the enduring value of these accumulated interactions.

A stable community with memories of past generations can become rigid and oppressive. The towns around me as a child were marked as either conservative or liberal. Every house had a paint stripe indicating the family's orientation. In fact, every house in a town would be the same color. Being a liberal or conservative in the wrong town could get you killed. Conformity based on fears could be tyrannical.

When people live together for many generations in the same town or region it becomes obvious that some ways of life do not turn out well and should be avoided. Some families stay poor, conflicted or rich but hated while others seem resilient when things go wrong. Towns and regions develop reputations of their own for the patterns that inhabit those ecosystems. Cultural and family patterns that develop over many generations explain and influence how life works. My grandchildren do not recognize the patterns that were a natural part of life for millennia.

However, understanding cause and effect has never been a clean and accurate process. My father was taught in science class that "spontaneous generation" was a fact and that electricity flowed from positive to negative. Eventually we discover that much of what we believed, taught and used to guide us was flawed and incorrect.

We cannot assume that there was only superstition, ignorance and rigidity in the human patterns that lasted for millennia. Unless we have observed the context and the effects of those patterns in life, families and cultures we do not see their long-term effects. The communities that allowed for long-term observations were part of my early life but have now largely disappeared. It has become apparent that what is disappearing most quickly is a sense of how past communities took care of future generations.

This book contains the observations and wisdom I have accumulated by looking into disappearing ways of life in places where families lived in the same house for generations, were not distracted by most of what happened in the rest of the world, never watched video screens and focused their attention on people. Focusing on people could be both kind and cruel but is was everywhere. These interaction patterns were intended to develop the best people in future generations – meaning those who could sustain and propagate the group identity for generations.

In these multi-generational human communities, gender development formed a key aspect of maturity. Gender interactions have been observed for millennia across many cultures, conditions and (very recently in human development) through scientific studies. When I wrote this book more than two decades ago there was nothing controversial about describing these genders as male and female – men and women. Interactions between men and women would start and shape each generation.

The links between gender, heterosexual activity and multiple generations are obvious. Multi-generational communities have always been centrally heterosexual. According to the Center for Disease Control (CDC) statistics for 2019 most children (84.4%) in schools identify as heterosexual.[1] What they need for their development into a sustainable, multi-generational community is the topic of this book series.

The assumption seems to be that becoming a well-adapted heterosexual is uncomplicated and will simply happen. The current grade school insult for a child expressing a heterosexual inclination is to call them "plain." Quite the contrary, there are complex demands

[1] https://www.cdc.gov/healthyyouth/data/yrbs/2019_tables/students_by_sexual_identity.htm
2.5% of school children identify as gay or lesbian, 8.7% as bisexual, and 4.5% as not sure. No science I am aware of can predict the outcome of current practices for children labeled as LGBTQ or their families over the next three or four generations. How to best parent children who identify as LGBTQ, is not the subject of this book, and no element or statement in this book should be taken as the way to raise them.

around being raised as a heterosexual person. Raising well-adjusted heterosexuals is extremely difficult to do and very demanding of community resources. Producing heterosexuals who can form life-long, secure attachments that are life-giving under strain, adaptable to change, good for both genders, protective against abuse or exploitation and high-joy for at least the following three generations is not easily achieved.

Maturity has never been easily developed and the objective of joyful communities with attachments that last a lifetime and longer has all but disappeared. Failures as partners, mates, parents and grandparents by immature heterosexual people are well known and documented. Many of these failures can only be considered criminal abuses. While working in a clinic where 1,200 appointments by sexually abused women and children were seen each month, we found that the majority of perpetrators were male. My experience has been that men contribute disproportionately to lowering the joy of communities, women and children. Men need a little more redemption than women so I will have more to say about them in this series.

We cannot conclude that heterosexual women will automatically develop healthy relationship patterns with men or children. The marriage counselors in our clinic had all the work they could handle helping women. My caseload covered the severe cases of men and women sexually abused by their mothers. The percentage of those sexually abused by women was much lower than the percentage abused by men. However, the number of boys sexually abused by women rose considerably when the same acts (such as exposing themselves) were deemed sexually abusive when performed by women. However, most people just said the boys were "lucky."

For over thirty years I have encouraged women to develop a comparable book to guide women's contributions to a multi-generational community. I doubt the best path will be making women's lives more like men's lives have been. Since status, power, career success, education, sexual aggression and greed can increase the relational failure rate for men I doubt those traits will reduce the relational failure rate among women.

Specialized focus: Both men and women are the core participants in a multi-generational community structure designed for lifelong attachments. A great deal of specialization and skill is required to keep a community joyful. This harmony requires well timed developmental training and experience. There is simply not enough time to get good at everything.

At a brain level, specialization in *something* means reducing our capacity to do *everything*. The brains of first time fathers raising children lose brain matter in the interpersonal region of the right temporal lobe.[1] First time fathers become faster and better at certain interpersonal tasks at the expense of keeping all their options open. The brains of first time fathers are trimmed to a limited number of quick responses like, "He probably needs to be changed so I will check his diaper."

For men who are not fathers, a baby's cry could bring up many options: "Whose baby is that? Why do babies have to cry so loud? Who is going to take care of it? Where are there quieter places to sleep?" The options are endless. Learning cogent responses trims unneeded brain options.

Specialized patterning: In addition to limiting options, the brain must learn social patterns that are easily recognized and produce expected responses from others. Let's say we would like a child to be a great gymnast. We would not leave the child to discover if gymnastics exists. When a child heard of gymnastics we would not leave them to make up their own moves or practice whatever they imagined the sport might be in order to become a winning, graceful and uninjured Olympic gymnast by age eighteen. Instead, coaches start by training a very limited number of specific gymnastic activities. Complex skills are built upon the basics. Proficiency at basic patterns is needed for all professional sports. The same is true for music, education and human relations.

The relational patterns needed for attachment and sustainable relationships across genders are much more complex and difficult than sports and music. Leaving children to invent their own patterns sets the child up to fail. They cannot match what has been discovered over millennia that could impact them or the next several generations if they get it wrong. Neither will others easily recognize and synchronize with what they are trying to achieve without standard social patterns.

The limitations and drawbacks of early training and specialization in gender roles and heterosexual identities are well known. Rigid and abusive restrictions have been imposed on gender roles to the detriment of individuals and future generations. When gender or sexual activity

---

[1] Magdalena Martínez-García, María Paternina-Die, Sofia I Cardenas, Oscar Vilarroya, Manuel Desco, Susanna Carmona, Darby E Saxbe, First-time fathers show longitudinal gray matter cortical volume reductions: evidence from two international samples, *Cerebral Cortex*, 2022; bhac333, https://doi.org/10.1093/cercor/bhac333

becomes tied to status the results become harmful for lower status people. Like all training, there are injuries to participants that must be carefully minimized. Many cultural training methods cause harm, in my view, through fear motivation, toxic shame, dominance, lack of protection and forced utility. Inability to use emotions to form better relationships and find our best identities is the common outcome.

Specialization deadlines: Basic patterns must be learned and practiced to develop adequate skills before they are needed. To be on a team in the World Cup, World Series, or Stanley Cup won't happen if we wait until age thirty to watch our first game. Mastery comes from training at the right age using specialized patterns and focus needed for success.

The brain also has critical periods for development. The two central periods of the brain's automatic selective trimming happen near age four and age thirteen. Neural pruning, parcellation and apoptosis are biologically programmed to specialize the brain at and selectively limit our options for mastery. Systematic brain training must take place early in life to anticipate the results of brain trimming. Waiting to train heterosexual social development until after these severe brain pruning stages greatly limits the capacity for successful mastery of heterosexual relationships. And it is not simply pruning that lies ahead as we mature. After age thirteen, brain development is strongly impacted by huge increases in the hormones irritating our nerves by their chemical presence. Any relational patterns we hope will run smoothly would need to be well established ahead of time.

How are we to provide the necessary training to grow sustainable multi-generational communities while avoiding the hazards and abuses documented for centuries in many different cultures? How can we retain what worked well in the past during the changes made by virtual cultures in the twenty-first century? I offer my observations about maturity and how it may be developed as part of growing a more human community together.

Jim Wilder 2024

Chapter One
The Goal

Hot chicken soup saved my life. The wind twisted over a low ridge and both rocks that stood between me and Iceberg Lake. Hidden in my high-tech sleeping bag, I was shaking uncontrollably from hypothermia. "What am I doing out here with this idiot?" I kept saying to myself.

About a thousand feet above me, flashlights provided security for two climbers roped for the night to a sheer rock face across very thin air from the Keeler Needle. Alfonse handed me the hot soup even as its warmth ebbed away. "Who could believe he was on the Sierra Madre Search and Rescue team," I thought. I was too exhausted to speak.

One full day, and 3,000 feet below, the North Fork of Lone Pine Creek splashed across the last spot I had seen of the Mt. Whitney Trail. There, at 8,800 feet, Alfonse had pointed me up the mountaineer's route along the left side of North Fork Creek. In a few minutes all traces of the trail had disappeared.

"We should be here," Alfonse said, looking at his topographical or "topo" map. He had climbed this face of the mountain before, so I followed him up the stream. We could see from the map that the trail would cross the stream again.

After an hour, the gorge narrowed to the width of the stream. "We should be here," Alfonse said. Left with no way but up, we climbed the cliff, a difficult effort with external-frame backpacks and no ropes. Whitney gleamed gray and white in the distance above us as we dragged ourselves up a tree root to the rock ledge at the top of the gorge.

Making our way from ledge to boulder, we headed toward 10,000 feet where we hoped to find the trail as it met the stream again. Two hours of climbing over rocks brought us to a spot a few hundred feet above the stream. "We should be here," Alfonse said, looking at his "topo" map—but we weren't. It was about noon.

The granite behind our backs went up Pinnacle Ridge to Thor Peak and back down before it met the main Whitney Trail to the south. It would take the rest of the day to get out that way so we pushed ahead. We crossed the tree line and headed toward Iceberg Lake—not that we could see a lake.

About five-thirty that evening we located the mountaineer's trail on the other side of the stream. The genius of having the trail on that side became starkly clear as the cold granite slammed into the sky directly ahead of us on our side. To go anywhere, except back the way we had come, we needed to cross the stream.

There was exactly one way to cross. In front of us was a waterfall. Half way up the falls, a stone ledge jutted through the spray. On our side, this shelf was about twelve inches wide. It looked to be about half that wide where the dripping gray rock emerged from the far side of the stream.

"We should be here," Topo Man said, "Iceberg Lake should be right over this ridge."

"So the waterfall we are about to crawl across is the water flowing out of Iceberg Lake," I said to myself and the wind.

"We should be there in a half hour and make camp. We'll heat up some chicken soup." With that he began to inch sideways across the face of the falls holding onto rocks through the rushing water. In the long afternoon shadows, his backpack stuck out at an angle that seemed destined to pull him backwards into the remaining beam of sunlight. I hoped he didn't fall because he was carrying our only stove. We had split up the supplies for the trip so we each carried half of what we needed – I had the tent, he had the stove.

The water made a fantail off my boot as a knife of ice water cut off sensation in my hands. I felt for the ledge with my toes and leaned my face as close to the madly leaping wall of water as breathing would allow. Fortunately, the water was not very deep. The first twenty feet through the spray were uneventful. With about the length of my body to go, the ledge narrowed to three inches wide, moss appeared on a few rocks, and my fingers quit reporting to my brain. I made a clear decision not to go back the same way.

Five minutes later, the wind off Iceberg Lake bit me in the face. Around me, and behind all the big rocks, was a group of ten climbers in their tents and sleeping bags. I couldn't walk any farther—I was shaking too hard. I fumbled to get my sleeping bag off and open. Alfonse opened his pack to make the soup.

"Hmmm. Smells like gas in here," he said. He pulled out the Primus and shook it. "Yup! Out of gas. It's all over my clothes."

I didn't care. "Well, refill it. Let's get some soup."

Alfonse looked uncomfortable, "I thought one tankful would last the trip," he said. "I didn't bring a refill." I was speechless. My internal map said, "You are here," pointing to high danger.

Was it rage, fear, cold or exhaustion that made me shake so hard the rock next to me seemed to move? I was out of options. After a long time, Alfonse wandered back into camp with hot soup. "Here you go!" he said, all smiles. "Some guy let me use his stove."

There is no better soup in the world than that cup of instant chicken soup. *Life soup* I called it. Now and keep a packet in the cupboard, at all times, in case of emergency. After a while I stopped shaking.

When I next discovered I was alive, it was morning. Iceberg Lake was covered with ice, clearly indifferent to the demands of August. The wind carried with it a complete explanation. I chipped a spot and got water.

The trail we had wanted went up the right-hand side of North Fork Creek. We missed the trail by fifteen feet when we headed up the left-hand bank. From then on, we were never where we should have been. With the help of a map, we eventually got back on the trail but I might have died anyway were it not for those who were there ahead of us. I had trusted an unreliable guide and traveled unprepared. From then on, when in the High Sierra, I carried everything needed for survival in my pack. I was always prepared and knew where I was.

=====

The phone rang and I answered it, as I hate to do. A man introduced himself. "Hi. This is Billy Solomon. My wife says I need to talk to you." We set an appointment for the next day.

Billy walked into the office wearing work boots and sat on the edge of the couch. "I'm goin' to kill the 'son-of-the-perverse-rebellious-woman,'[1]" he said. "My wife is sleeping with some snake and she tells *me* to get counseling," Billy was shaking so hard that he couldn't sit still. He half-fell and half-leapt off the couch and rushed to the window.

[1] King James Version translation. See 1 Samuel 20:30.

I thought he might go through it. "She is the only woman I ever loved, Doc!" He stood there trembling, then spread the mini-blinds with two fingers and stared out the hole. "Where am I?" he whispered hoarsely. "How did I get here?"

"This is going to take more than chicken soup," I thought.

He was thinking, "What am I doing here with this idiot!" To me he said, "No offense Doc, but how are *you* going to help me get her back?"

Billy's maturity was somewhere in early childhood while his life's trail was somewhere in mid-fatherhood. Like so many men, he had no idea what had just happened to him. He had worked at the same garage for sixteen years. He paid the bills, kept the kids in line, and took the family on vacation each year. He had made a way through the mountains of his life and was stepping from just another ledge to just another boulder when something in his wife gave way. Now, next to my window, Billy's hand raked down the mini-blinds as his arms dropped. Shaking uncontrollably, he registered signs of shock.

=====

Maybe in a gorge or when the trail disappears; high on a ridge or after a near fall; when a bear gets our food or when the sun is setting; we look around and ask the wind, "Where am I?"

Well, here is a map. We will trace the trail starting from birth. Since you are old enough to read this, you are also old enough to have been off the trail by now—not just once but many times. Like Alfonse, we often think "we should be here"—but we are not. I've prepared this book as a "topo" map for those who are lost. I've included a supply list for those who are planning trips for themselves—or their families. But, a few of us are in real danger. We will die tonight unless we find a fellow climber, with a working stove, to give us *LIFE soup*.

Let's begin looking for the little arrow that says "*You* are *here*." Where you are *now* is where you must start. Any rescue or growth starts right here. You cannot be someone else or someplace else. Life is here—or nowhere. We can't memorize a trail to follow because each day the trail changes. Our goal is to live for each step, whether on the trail or off. When we do, we get someplace.

THE LIFE CYCLE FROM BIRTH TO DEATH

The world's languages reflect an intuitive sense about maturity. Every language I know has a word for a baby, child, adult, parent and elder. For millennia we have passed through these stages and transformations.

At each stage more is expected and that development requires the learning, practice and judgment we call maturity.

Teaching about maturity around the USA allowed me to watch people assess their personal maturity. About three out of four men I encountered functioned at the infant level of maturity. Infant maturity is not the same as infant age. These men are well beyond the infant age but how well they knew themselves revealed infant issues were not clarified or resolved. We will have much to say about these infant needs and tasks. Our goal is reaching the maturity that matches our age.

Infant maturity tasks focus on developing a clear sense of *ME* and what I need. Men, or anyone at infant maturity, will need examples that fit them fairly exactly. If I use an example that is "not me" for someone at infant maturity the application is quickly rejected. Boys will reject examples that are "for girls" or any kind of person they do not identify with themselves.

I discovered that women were more often at child maturity and able to apply an idea that was illustrated with a male example to themselves. In addition, male examples helped women recognize maturity (or the lack of it) in men. By recognizing infant maturity quickly we are less likely depend on men like Alfonse or Billy.

Because so few men mature past the infant stage, they need a clear trail to follow. This book provides clear pictures of what male maturity requires at each stage in order to keep up with brain development and become a sustaining member of a multi-generational community.

Over my lifespan the average level of maturity in the USA has seem to drop rather than rise. Maturity is a people skill and best acquired and developed through practice with people. Time spent interacting with screens rather than people is increasing. In addition, we are increasingly mobile and every time we move we lose some part of our relational world.

We need maturity maps and skill practice to successfully raise children to be adults, partners, parents and elders at the same rate that we age. We need to know what pace to set and what pace is sustainable. Our maturity will lag if we follow guides who do not know the way or lack the skills to get us there. Life, like mountain terrain, can present very different challenges at different stages. Let us consider some of the identity goals we reach by growing *ME* (an individual), *US* (a family) and *WE* (a community).

THE FIRST GOAL: BABY

The first major challenge for growing *ME* begins at birth and lasts until about age four. Babies must receive grace – the certain knowledge that they are special. Parents and community look at a baby's unformed identity through the eyes of heaven and watch what will grow there.

In chapter two we will examine all the experiences needed at this INFANT STAGE. These first four years are the baby years. Babies need to receive all good things and learn to express themselves. Each baby learns the value of "just being me" without having to earn value.

Ideally, babies learn all the basics of self-care. Later skills will build upon these basics. Many babies will not be taught to grow their relational self properly. Key self-care skills are often omitted. Abuse and neglect create an entirely wrong sense of who their *self* is and what a *self* needs.

Infants must experience strong, loving, caring bonds with parents. These bonds must meet their needs without babies having to ask. Infants must receive life, and learn to express the life that is in them, to everyone's delight. During infancy babies learn to live joyfully in the protected environment of a mother's world.

A baby's identity will either be built around joy or fear. The infant whose brain "backpack" is filled with joy becomes strong. Joyful babies will not fear the trails or mountains. Keeping baby from beginning a life of fear requires breaking life into baby-sized pieces. Each effort leads to letting baby rest in a timely way. The baby years are synchronized to baby's needs.

When life comes in baby size, infants learn to synchronize and control their minds and emotions. They learn to quiet themselves and soon are ready to synchronize with others. Relationships that are both joyful and peaceful result from getting this timing right. Video screens do not provide this joy and rest training.

Four years of infancy prepares babies for weaning. In our culture, weaning from the breast or bottle is rarely timed to coincide with when the child is ready for self-care. We rush our children into independence as fast as possible. Weaning from infancy changes a baby into a child. Once babies have learned to take basic care of their needs, they can transform into children who can begin living a less sheltered life in their father's world. Children move from life in their home toward life in both home and community.

It may well be that many infants and children no longer experience either a mother's world or a father's world and cannot distinguish the differences that have existed through human history between the two. Some thought should be given to whether this recent change in child rearing is contributing to the rapid increase of insecure attachments, depression, fragility, isolation and anxiety in young adults of the 21st century.[1]

Reaching where we should be on the maturity trail begins where we actually are. Without the experiences we needed it is inevitable that our maturity will get stuck in infancy. Missing maturity does not mean we lack value, it just feels that way if our infant need for grace went unmet. To correct deficits and build successive maturity stages we must go back to learn what we missed. No one likes to be called a "baby" or an "infant" when they are older so it is hard to pick a name for this stage that doesn't offend us later when we think of remediation.

The goal for infancy is for babies to organize a strong, joyful, synchronized identity.

THE SECOND GOAL: CHILD

The CHILD STAGE begins as the baby becomes a child at about age four. Once weaned, and able to begin self-care, children can become quite upset if they are called babies. Even in their own minds a transformation has taken place. We will explore the child's world in chapter seven.

A child is more complex than a baby. Children must learn to ask for the things they need. They must make themselves understandable to others. Children must discover what satisfies them each day. To do this, each child must learn to act exactly like themselves—like the identity in that child's heart. Children must develop their talents and resources. Their performance must be self-expression but not as a way to earn love. Children must learn to receive and give life freely. They must learn to do hard things, things that they don't feel like doing at the time, but which are important and satisfying later. Each child learns how to pack and carry their own backpack, read a map, keep moving on the trail and enjoy the view.

In preparation for adulthood, children learn the "big picture" of life. This overall picture of life and maturity becomes their "topo" map. The

[1] Konrath SH, Chopik WJ, Hsing CK, O'Brien E. Changes in adult attachment styles in American college students over time: a meta-analysis. Pers Soc Psychol Rev. 2014 Nov;18(4):326-48. doi:10.1177/1088868314530516. Epub 2014 Apr 12. PMID: 24727975.

history of their own family will illustrate how the big picture of life applies to people they know. Who has matured? Who has some obvious gaps? Family history tells them where *ME* is on *my* map.

The goal for childhood is to teach children to take care of one person—themselves. Children learn to participate in life with grace by being special in the company of special people. Children learn to see themselves through the eyes of heaven and cultivate what is growing within them. Taking care of self must be second nature before they can take care of two or more people at the same time, as adults must do.

THE THIRD GOAL: ADULT

Ideally, the ADULT STAGE begins at age thirteen. Many in the Boomer generation set a goal of never growing up to be adults only to lament the lack of adults in subsequent generations. Growing an adult identity is the topic of the second book in the *Growing a More Human Community* series. We will look at adult maturity in ADULTS: *Growing Us*. Like other transformations, becoming an adult is physical as well as mental and social. A young adult's identity will try to reorganize itself but without an older guide, it will end up in a disorganized state.

It takes a while to climb the many peaks that separate a self-centered child from a both-centered adult. A mature child can take excellent care of one person, themselves. Given the necessary guidance, young adults can satisfy the needs of more than one person at a time. Adult terrain is where one learns to drive a hard bargain, fair for oneself and fair for the other. Adults protect the needs of others as though they were as important as their own. When adults do business, the person they are dealing with gets equal, fair treatment. This stage of development usually takes people into their early twenties. By that time, adults should be able to bargain hard, get a fair deal, not be intimidated by others, protect others from themselves when necessary and take care of a small group to everyone's satisfaction.

Adults want their effects to reflect their personal character and style. Everything they do must meet this heart-based standard. Adults share grace by making sure everyone is treated as special. Adults learn to see others through the eyes of heaven in order to grow the best group identity. Any group, such as a family or church, where the preponderance of participants have not reached adult maturity will be dysfunctional. Without the eyes of heaven the group will not be transformative and lapse into raising their own status through performance and image management.

Adult identity finds its highest challenge in marriage. People are ready for marriage near the end of the adult stage. By that time they are proficient in sharing life for mutual satisfaction. Because the two are both adults, they can each take care of themselves and others simultaneously. This kind of partnership is characteristically adult. Sharing life in a way that creates a mutually satisfying story—or imprint on history—brings great joy to adults.

The goal for adults is to become a satisfying part of history. Adults know they impact other people. Therefore, adults carefully insure that their impact on history (my story) is a good one.

THE FOURTH GOAL: PARENT

The PARENT STAGE uses all we have learned in the first three stages to reach our highest peak—giving life. Parents already know what they need and feel. Parents look out for others like they do for themselves. They now learn to give without receiving in return, as we will see in second book of this set called ADULTS: *Growing Us.*

We know that we are parents when our child keeps us up all night, screaming in our ear, spitting up on our shirts and then showing no appreciation for our efforts. We could have bargained hard, like adults, and said, "I'll stay up with you tonight but tomorrow night you must carry me around," but we didn't. Instead we gave without demanding in return. This is the mountain peak we have trained for all our lives. As we start this ascent, we know we are parents.

Let's say that the father stays up this time. The father knows what he needs. He already reached his infant goals. No one stays up all night and says, "I never need to sleep." He can express his feelings about it as well, "I'm tired but I love my child." He can take care of himself in the morning using the skills he learned as a boy. If and when his wife takes over, both are satisfied with the baby's care. Although at work he drives a hard bargain, at home he climbs above the tree line into unselfish giving. Only a mature person who has completed the first three stages can enjoy the climb.

Parents give grace, the sense of being special, to their children. Parents see their children through the eyes of heaven rather than through their own needs and expectations. Parents pass on the gift of grace by unselfish giving. Children learn about having value without having to earn it. By staying up all night a parent says, "My child, you have great value to me. Even if you keep me up all night, spit up on me, mess in your diapers and scream in my ear, even if you do not care that I am here, you have more than enough value to lose sleep over." That is parent maturity.

Parents represent God to their family. The chance to portray God is the greatest honor that anyone can have. The parent becomes an example of God's heart and character through unselfish giving. This takes a while, and parents are getting the hang of it about the time the children become teens. By that time, unselfishness should be second nature to Mom and Dad – they will need it.

To be a giver of life, a parent must have received enough life to spare some. Parents must share a home where they can protect, serve and enjoy. They must find the resources that allow their children to mature.

The goal of parenthood is to give life joyfully. As parents give life, children grow strong.

THE FIFTH GOAL: ELDER

Although many an older person has illustrated the need for more maturity, not much has been written about how seniors develop elder maturity at their age. We will study the ELDER STAGE in volume three of this series titled SENIORS: *Growing We the People.*

After their children have become adult men and women, a truly *grand*-parent becomes a guide. Elders help those who are climbing for the first time. They rescue those who didn't bring maps, forgot their supplies, or even got lost. Elders give life to the "familyless"—the widows, orphans and strangers. They help their community to mature and reach its identity.

Many people could use an elder or a *grand*parent. In our society we expect older people to buy a motorhome and drive into the sunset. We, therefore, have few elders, few spare parents, few guides and few people helping those in need. There is a great lack of elders in our churches and communities.

An elder is a parent to a community. Elders see their community's group identity through the eyes of heaven. God and God's people both know and see what is special in others. Elders help those who have no one who sees them as special to discover grace. Elders provide the same unselfish care for those who are not biologically their children as they gave their own families. They remind everyone what kind of people we are and what we value.

Cohesion is built by elders because they live transparent lives. They no longer hide what they feel so they can be "cool." They are real in ways they haven't been since they were children. They do not give self-protection the highest value because they have learned to suffer well. Elders don't withdraw when things go wrong because they know how often people fail to live from their hearts. Elders are steady in good times and bad. Through authentic involvement, elders resynchronize their community from its broken relationships, failures and failed trust. Elders may not do much of the actual community repair work but they help others get their timing right. "This is not the time for that," they say and then again, "this is the time to do something else."

Elders must have a community of their own, a place where each elder is recognized and encouraged. Elders must be given a proper place in the community structure for they will not force their way. We need guides who have been to the mountain. Old mountaineers die when they have no one to guide.

"I know just what you need," must echo again in the canyons.

When elders die, it is a time of great blessing. Every elder prepares to face the greatest human transformation—a plunge into Iceberg Lake. This is the final decontamination process from all that may have gone wrong on their journey. Everything about elders that received and gave life emerges beyond Iceberg Lake. Anything about them that gave death stays in the lake forever.

The goal for elders is to help their community grow up. Elders raise communities the way parents raise children. Under elders, communities reach their full maturity.

=====

If I had my way about it, I'd forget this book and have each of you sit with elders and learn to see yourself through the eyes of heaven. They would serve you hot *LIFE soup*. With their help you would find your own level of maturity, get outfitted, reach the trail again, and climb your mountain.

THE FIRST METAMORPHOSIS

*

THE INFANT (BABY) STAGE

*

RECEIVING GRACE

BABY

The Infant Stage

IDEAL AGE
Birth through Three

NEEDS
- Strong, loving, caring bonds with parents
- Important needs are met without asking
- Others take the lead and synchronize with baby first
- Quiet together time
- Help regulating distress and emotions
- Being seen through the "eyes of heaven"
- Receiving and giving life

•

TASKS
- Receiving with joy
- Learn to synchronize with others
- Organize himself into a person through imitation
- Learn to regulate and quiet every emotion
- Learn how to return to joy from every emotion
- Learn to be the same person over time
- Learn self-care skills
- Learn to rest

•

Chapter Two
Baby Learns Joy

*A woman giving birth to a child has pain because her time has come; but when her baby is born she forgets the anguish **because of her joy** that a child is born into the world.*

Jesus (John 16:21 NIV)

The celebration that greets a baby's birth gives us a felt-sense of how that life will go. What a good thing has happened!

"It's a boy!" A nurse spoke the first words over me. "What a schnazola!" she said. Words to live by, I would think. Perhaps that was the beginning of my becoming a well-bonded individual because, as we will soon see, bonding starts with the nose.

"It's a girl!" Tomorrow we will want to know how many ounces she has lost, and the day after that how many she has gained. The measuring of her progress is well under way. She is completely an infant and yet so much less than a baby must become.

"Here is your baby!" Babies are products of the history that went before them. That history will shape many things including their names. All the same, each baby is an enigma at birth because their very birth has started history in a different direction. No one knows where it will lead. New fathers and mothers can feel overwhelmed at that potential and need.

"It's a boy!" That once meant blue clothes and shopping in auto parts stores. On the average, boys receive far fewer offers to hold a baby or sew a dress. People say fewer words to him during his infancy than if he were a girl. He will generally be left out of discussions about mascara. We have ideas as a culture that will shape his growth. Our ideas change but the inevitability that our ideas will impact a baby's formation does not change.

"It's a girl!" Hopeful girls are the foundation of cultural advancement.[1] What makes girls hopeful is the way that babies are valued and how women and girls are treated in their cultures. Hopeful girls grow up to raise joyful children, full of creativity, that drive positive social growth.

Liverpool was a very dreary place after World War II. As a port city, the social environment was dominated by strong women who understood life and raised the children. Many local men were sailors who visited their families periodically when in port. These sailors sometimes brought home exciting discoveries and music from afar. Four lads from town heard this imported music and came up with a plan to create joyful excitement for girls using music. In turn, joyful girls made the Beatles a world phenomenon.

Babies are born ready for joy. They will amplify the joy around them. Good parents build joy. Joy is the brain's way to say, "I'm glad to be with you!" Neither parents nor baby have much idea of who is inside the faces they are greeting with glad smiles.

Parents anticipate that the unknown promise in each baby will be valuable and special. No performance is needed from their baby. The joy of being together creates the right conditions for discovering the ME that heaven sees in a child if parents, family and community provide the necessary experiences.

THE INFANT AT BIRTH

Becoming a baby—INFANT is the first stage. The baby's task is creating a working identity from whatever happens the next four years. The first half of this stage we usually consider as "baby" and the second half as "toddler" but we will use "baby" or "infant" to describe the entire first four years of life. The goal of infancy is growing a synchronized self that moves with our body's rhythms and fits well with the people around us. Babies must work through this difficult process, learning as they go about what they need and who they are.

My friend Chris came to see me one day in 1997. He is an unusually sensitive man who had learned to have interactive thought exchanges with God.

"God wants me to tell you that he created little kids with lots of be-like stuff," Chris said.

---

[1] Lloyd deMause, Childhood and Cultural Evolution, The Journal of Psychohistory, Vol 26, #3, Winter 1999, page 642-723.

"What is bee-like stuff?" I asked him. I could not make any sense out of his statement. Had it been almost anyone else, I would have suggested trying some medication. But, Chris had a good track record.

"You know, something to help them be-like other people, something that lets them take the shape of people around them, to be like them. Little kids grow to be like their parents. That is how they were made."

Two years later I was introduced to lectures by Dr. Allan Schore, a well known expert on the development of children's brains. Schore commented that the part of the brain that contains a baby's identity begins growing at three months of age. How this identity grows is the most interesting part. A baby tracks and imitates a mature brain (usually mother) until the baby has copied how the bigger brain thinks and feels. This identity area, known as the prefrontal cortex, becomes 35% of the adult brain. That is a lot of be-like stuff!

A baby is a sponge, or maybe more of a vacuum cleaner, sucking in everything it can from bigger brains. A baby becomes what a baby receives. Receiving comes before giving. It is part of our dependency on God and others that we never outgrow.

Even Jesus started out receiving. It seems to bother some Christmas storytellers that all we have recorded about Jesus as an infant is that he received from others. There are no miracles for little drummer boys, no healings, no dividing his lunch among 5,000 people. While the traditional carol says that while in the manger the little Lord Jesus did not cry, there is no support for that theory. He would have expressed needs and feelings and then received from others what he did not earn.

Babies eventually learn to express needs with words. By the time infancy is over, every baby should have mastered expressing both needs and feelings and then receiving without shame—but a cow could do that! To be human requires more. It is the joyful relationship between the one who gives and the one who receives that make us alive. A babies' brain comes to be-like whoever provides joy.

BECAUSE OF JOY

Understanding babies requires us to understand joy. Being human and wanting relational joy are inseparable. We humans are creatures of joy. We like joy. We seek joy. We never outgrow our desire for relational joy. Joy is even characteristic of our eternal existence. God makes "everlasting joy" a promise for his people through the prophet Isaiah; and who would not want it? (Isaiah 51:11)

At its essence, joy is relational. Joy is the delight we experience when someone really connects with us. They want to be with us and we with them. Our faces glow. Our eyes grow big and sparkle. We smile and laugh and our hearts and senses open wide to gather them into us. Joy means someone is with me and I like it!

Joy is present even before birth. In the Bible story of the birth of Jesus, Elizabeth tells Mary, "the babe leaped in my womb for joy," (Luke 1:44b KJV) making joy the youngest recorded emotion in scripture. Joy is also the first emotion that infants will seek on their own. Seeking joy is the primary, and perhaps strongest, sustainable human motivation. Joy is the centerpiece of human personality and brain structure. In fact, joy and the search for joy form the basis for all healthy bonding.[1]

Joy is what we feel when someone is glad to see us. When their face lights up, we feel joy. We are loved, enjoyed, appreciated, served and protected and it gives us joy. Our eyes want to look to them. Our feet want to run to them. We want to jump, skip, dance and sing. Joy is being with someone who is glad to be with us.

It is very painful if we are ignored, hurt or exploited during our search for joy. Many bad and confusing outcomes are generated. *ME* becomes damaged and usually becomes "bad." We begin developing an "as-if me," an avatar behind which to hide. These performance based avatars will later take on a life of their own. What we really want is someone who is glad to be with *ME*.

Mothers are usually a baby's biggest joy. If we picture the adventure of raising a child as though it were learning to camp, then a mother's first goal would be setting up a base camp at the foot of Mount Joy. *Joy Camp* would be our place to live and grow strong. It would be the place to build a strong, joyful identity. All our expeditions would begin from Joy Camp and end when we got back to Joy Camp.

JOY CAMP

The first three months of life are devoted to establishing Joy Camp as the base of operations. During those twelve weeks a baby feels joy from being close to mother. Activities like nursing, rocking, sleeping near the baby or carrying the infant near her body are very beneficial. This joyful state is the root of all human development. Living in Joy Camp is the basis for understanding mother-love, home, belonging, peace, security and all our treasured experiences. No matter how far we may roam in

[1] Allan Schore, Affect Regulation and the Origin of the Self, (Hillsdale, NJ: Lawrence Erlbaum Associates Publishers, 1994) pp 83-91.

our lifetime, Joy Camp is where we wish we were each night as we fall asleep.

During the first half of our time in Joy Camp our joy comes from mother's smell, from being fed and staying warm.[1] These three experiences bring joy and create the beginning bond between mother and infant. Particular attention is needed to make sure the baby's needs are met when nursing so that the baby can be joyful and bond. Parent or clock-controlled feeding schedules are destructive at this age. Eating and regulating their own temperatures are new skills for babies. Any success with those two tasks brings rest for the first six weeks of life. Failure blocks and may even damage nerve endings in the developing brain.

Smell is the first sense to be used for bonding because it is the best developed sense at birth. Baby could smell mother in the womb and only mother smells that way. Babies and mothers both use this sense to identify each other. There is a lot of "baby sniffing" between mothers and their newborns.

It may be wise to keep the baby's life free from artificial smells during the first six weeks when bonding is largely by smell. One wonders what effect smells can have at this age. For instance, what if mother smells of alcohol or tobacco? Bonding with cigarette smoke or alcohol on the parents' breath, the smell of fresh paint in the baby room, or perfumes may include these smells among those which will say comfort, love and belonging for the baby's whole life. Under stress they will seek these smells for comfort. One mother helped her children by giving them each a small bottle of the perfume she had worn during their infancy as they left home.

Our life-long goal becomes returning to Joy Camp each and every night. Just as salmon go back in search of the smell of the place where they were hatched, we go back seeking the smell of Joy Camp. Smells become a way to repair bad days. That might not be totally bad if we head toward mother, baby powder, baby oils, or even fresh paint, but seeking alcohol, tobacco, or chasing perfumed women who smoke might be.

Two different women with severe early bonding problems and inability to regulate their emotions have told me that during their first year of therapy with me they went to stores smelling all the deodorants trying to locate the one I used so that they could have my "smell" with

---

[1] Ibid p. 106. Also Schore, Affect Dysregulation and the Disorders of the Self, (New York, NY: W. W. Norton and Co. 2003) p. 7.

them. Although they both were very ashamed of themselves for invading my privacy, their growing confidence of a return to Joy Camp let them tell me. In both cases they had located the correct brand—a generic product not available in most stores.

The second phase that establishes Joy Camp is touch centered. After six weeks, the touch centers of the baby's brain are developed enough for touch to become the strongest sense. From six to twelve weeks, touch becomes the main source of infant joy. This new awareness is possible because the baby's developing brain is now able to sort out and remember skin sensations. Without touch, as with other stressful conditions, a baby's body will generate cortisol—a stress hormone that will literally kill off some brain cells.

Through smell, taste, temperature and touch babies come to understand themselves as ME in relationship to mother. That is why eating when baby is hungry, being touched when baby needs to be held, being able to find and smell mother are so important. This is Joy Camp. Parents make baby feel good. Important needs are met without asking. A strong, loving, caring bond is growing with parents as babies begin to organize themselves into human beings.

By three months babies have developed their minds enough to start picturing what mother feels about them. From three months on joy becomes very interactive. Now the baby is ready to attempt the seemingly impossible task of teaching his or her brain to be like the parents' brains. Until now the baby's capacity to feel joy has been very small and easily filled. After three months the main joy structures in the brain begin their serious growth spurt.[1] What is growing is the fast track in baby's right brain that runs faster than conscious thought.

CLIMBING JOY MOUNTAIN

Joy is very relational thus the way joy forms our identity is relational as well. Our deepest sense of self forms in relationship to a face looking at us. By studying this face and eyes we know what they feel about us. Our self-concept develops from how we think others see us. Babies take all these facial expressions personally. A sad face means, "I make people sad," a glad face means, "I bring joy."

---

[1] For an extended discussion of neurobiological development in the infant see the trilogy of books by Dr. Allan N. Schore 1) Affect Regulation and the Origin of the Self 1994, 2) Affect Regulation and the Repair of the Self 2003 and 3) Affect Dysregulation and the Disorders of the Self 2003.

Babies develop a mental image of how their mother sees them. Not surprisingly it is stored, without words, as an image of her face. It is also no surprise that climbing Joy Mountain has to wait until the visual areas of the brain mature at two or three months of age. Fortunately, tired mothers have had two or three months to recover from giving birth before babies need their smiles. By then the visual cortex has been "hardwired" into place making vision the dominant sense. Babies look for eyes that are looking at them with joy. Joy means, "Someone is thrilled to see me."

Joy is the emotion that babies seek spontaneously. Nothing interests babies more than looking at faces and eyes. Whenever they see joyful eyes looking at them, the joy inside explodes. In a matter of five or six seconds they can be smiling and giggling—full of excitement and joy. Each time they see joyful eyes, a face that lights up to see them, they make another attempt to climb Joy Mountain.

Because they like high joy levels, babies keep seeking joy even when things go wrong. As they climb to higher and higher levels of joy, babies are building their brain's capacity to handle life. The capacity to experience strong joy develops between three and twelve months of age if baby has a parent's help.

Emotional regulation capacity grows incrementally as the infant attempts, repeatedly, to reach higher and higher levels of joy. By their first birthday, with lots of practice, they regularly reach the top of Joy Mountain and feel joy as powerfully as a human can! Hundreds of hours practicing joy with others grows a strong and joyful ME.

JOY AND THE HUMAN BRAIN

At two to three months of age a region of the brain, which was not developed at birth, begins its growth. This area, called the right prefrontal cortex (rPFC), will become the top of the command center in the brain. The rPFC has the last word on both body and mind systems. The rPFC grows to become about one sixth of the adult brain. It is the first to know everything from inside or outside the body. But this region is not an "it." In fact, these circuits grow as images of three faces (hopefully joyful) looking at each other—mother, baby and father. The strongest bond is usually between the mother and child face with the father looking at them both. This relational image of the self with joyful parents is stored as our identity at the top of a four-level control system of the brain.

We might wonder immediately, "Why am I not aware of these faces and points of view?" The answer is that they operate in the fast track of the brain that is faster than conscious thought. We are aware of who we are but we can never consciously "catch ourselves" figuring out who we are. We update who we are faster than we can consciously observe ourselves. Because the fast track is so fast, we always know I am *ME* before we can consciously observe the process. Because we cannot observe the fast track consciously but we can watch the slower conscious process, we tend to think that conscious thought is more important. Sometimes we make the mistake of thinking that our conscious mind is in charge of the brain and that is a huge mistake.

Our primary identity, at the apex of the neurological control structure of the brain, is a relational one. For the moment we will call this relational identity "*they*". If "*they*" are oriented by love we can bear all things, endure all things and return to joy. Joy is our strength. If "*they*" are oriented to fear then our identity readily becomes unstable and disorganized. Isn't it like God to design a brain that only knows itself correctly in relationship, and then only when that relationship is one of love? It is love that rejoices in knowing us that makes us know ourselves. This entire rPFC region is developed without words before the baby has a vocabulary. Its growth is nearly half over by the time we can say "mama."

ME, the control center for the self, is grown in response to mother's facial expressions and stored in the baby's brain as an image of mother's face. This visual image will interpret the meaning of my experiences and value of my identity. There is more than just my face and hers in the image. The rPFC is a three-way image of two people gazing at each other with a third face watching. Sometimes father and baby are close while mother watches. Sometimes baby watches mom and dad interact. Other faces can become the third face from time to time if they provide a harmony of expression.

The nature, style, rhythm and components of a relational ME are being developed before the baby is even speaking. These essential patterns become the fast-acting foundation for joy in a multi-generational world.

But why do I say "mother" instead of primary caretaker? Won't any person do? Only mother will smell like the bonding smell in the womb. Over human history, mothers have spent the most time with babies. Women's brains have larger and stronger joy centers (on average) compared to men. In addition, babies prefer to train for joy with those who have bigger brain centers if that person is bonded to the baby and shows an active interest. All the same, babies can adapt to many conditions much like we can eat all kinds of things and survive. What sustains us might still not be the best diet. One of my granddaughters reached fifteen years of age without eating a vegetable and she is quite active and bright.

Baby's attention will be drawn to the most intense face and eyes. She (or he) will match her face to theirs, her mind to theirs and grow her own copy of the strongest connection she finds. Let us hope she finds joy on all the faces. She will learn to be joyful like them. This will charge her inner being with joy. This will provide the strength she will use to fill her "backpack" for life's climb. Without relational joy strength her mind will fill with fear. It will be one or the other—fear or joy.

The prefrontal cortex has its main growth from three to eighteen months. But unlike the rest of the brain that gets "hardwired" and stops growing, the rPFC stays young all our lives. The joyful identity region in the right hemisphere undergoes growth spurts again at four and eight years of age, at the beginning of significant relationships and at the birth of one's child or grandchild. At these identity formation times, bonding is at its best. These are also the times when repairs can most easily be made to weak bonds. Often adopted children or those whose mothers were sick or working during their first brain growth time can form remedial attachments during these growth spurts. These are:

AGE	STAGE	FOCUS	OTHER
0-2 years	Early infant	Mother	Father
4 years	Early child	Father	Siblings, friends
8 years	Late child	Friends	Remedial
15 years	Early adult	First love—mate	Group identity
First child	Early parent	First baby	Remedial
Grandchild	Elder	First Grandchild	Remedial

The overwhelming euphoria that accompanies the growth of our "joyful identity control center" (in the fast track of the right prefrontal cortex) is what we felt with our first love, our first baby and our first grandchild. Looking in their eyes or seeing their smile threatens our brain with overload. Our brains flood with new nerve endings and the necessary brain chemistry needed for life such as serotonin, endorphins, and dopamine. On both sides of a joyful exchange the results are the same. Both brains are climbing Mt. Joy.

We are creatures of joy. Babies that do not see joy on their mothers' faces become full of fear. Babies also take in the upset feelings of others. If they attach to someone who is afraid, angry or distressed they learn to watch for threats. If they do not find eyes that are watching them with joy, they will not attach securely. If there is no one there at all, babies monitor the world looking for anything upsetting rather than expecting life to be joyful. They don't explore or even seek trails that lead back to joy. Monitoring constantly for threats is exhausting and soon the baby's control center becomes desynchronized. Now ME must spend most of my mental energy trying to keep my emotional equilibrium. ME lives by avoidance because ME has no hope of receiving help finding joy if something should go wrong. The brain develops fear driven motivation and a fear based identity.

Infants need someone who is paying attention to them and will help them feel better. As they grow older, people who never receive this loving bond are always searching for someone or something to make them feel better. In our culture this most often means drugs or sex, power or money.

Joy and strength
This capacity to feel joy at high levels achieves many purposes, but it is most clearly the source of personal strength. Our goal is to grow a strong ME. Babies "work out" by climbing Joy Mountain to develop a strong self or as psychologists call it "ego strength." As scripture says, "The joy of the Lord is your strength." (Nehemiah 8:10b KJV) In their ninth month babies will spend up to eight hours a day building their brains by smiling with their mothers. Mothers who get nothing done around the house and only "play" with their baby should know they are building their baby's brain and strength for life.

The strength of a human being is limited by how much joy we "pack" through life. Joy sustains us through suffering, illness, loss, mistakes, and disappointments. If we look at the people we know who have great joy, we discover they are very resilient – even under great hardship. Like the first century story of Paul and Silas singing their way back to joy in jail after being beaten, the person with joy is strong. Even when facing simple problems, like surviving in school, the child with joy is popular, attractive, and appealing.

People with little joy are often overwhelmed. Their personalities are weaker. Without vigorous workouts on Joy Mountain their brains are underdeveloped. Underdeveloped structures in the joyful identity area of the brain have been found in such diverse conditions as: depression, schizophrenia, attention deficit disorder, eating disorders, borderline personality and the autism spectrum. People with these conditions experience more difficulty maintaining joy. Some also experience difficulty recognizing facial expressions correctly. For instance, tired faces look angry so they are easily hurt and upset. They may not recover from upset feelings in a timely way. Their brain's control center becomes desynchronized and consequently their relationships and emotions can become unstable.

Climbing up and getting down
Ego strength is actually a capacity to regulate our own brains during high levels of emotional arousal. Learning regulation takes many repetitions. Since babies will only seek joy, it is the emotion we must use for training. Baby must learn to get to a high arousal state and then learn to calm back down voluntarily. Infants who can raise their energy and respond to life have "drive." Babies who can calm themselves when emotions heat up have poise and confidence. Climbing Joy Mountain and getting back down is how a baby learns these two opposing and essential tasks needed for a well-trained brain.

Rising joy generates dopamine and gives babies a chance to develop and control their dopamine system. Dopamine is a big part of our "go for it!" That sluggish, I-must-have-some-coffee feeling is low dopamine. We need to climb Joy Mountain more often.

Learning to quiet oneself and get back down Joy Mountain teaches a baby to develop and control the serotonin system. Serotonin is our "I'm fine" system. That irritable and unhappy, channel surfing, craving something, restless feeling is low serotonin. An inability to quiet ME contributes to addictions of all kinds. While babies don't seek to practice quieting, it is a natural part of the Joy Mountain experience. What goes up must come down. Babies need lots of repetitions.

Dopamine and serotonin are two of the brain's five chemical value systems. While the biology of the five value systems in the brain is very complex and little understood, training dopamine and serotonin produces a stable sense of ME. I can produce and control a natural joy high and bring it down to a natural calm. A baby learns both in the first year of life. Starting the second year of life babies will extend their serotonin control to quiet unpleasant feelings. We will look at these negative feelings later in this chapter.

More benefits of Joy Mountain

Until they develop a strong ME, babies will be overwhelmed by joy every time they get too high on Joy Mountain. Being overwhelmed feels like when we get tickled too much and can't stand it. Joy turns to pain as a baby reaches "overwhelmed." If a mother is using her baby to make herself happy she will keep trying to get them to smile and overwhelm them instead. A well-trained parent brain will notice that her baby has had too much joy and will look away for a moment to let them rest. When her baby looks back, the parent knows it is time to start climbing again.

Studies indicate that too much stimulation is even more harmful than not enough.[1] Alternating joy with resting quietly together allows babies to synchronize their own minds and relationships. So, to develop a well-coordinated brain the mother must synchronize her cycle of joy and rest to match the baby's need and capacity. Mother follows baby. As a result her baby learns to be energetic and calm which develops the emotional capacity for the baby to now synchronize with mother. Now baby follows mother.

This process is repeated thousands of times until baby can reach the top of Mt. Joy. But all these starts and stops on the way up bring hidden bonuses. Babies learn that they can survive being slightly overwhelmed, that they can recover by resting, and that they can return to joy. These steps, repeated many times, teach them how to regulate their own emotions. Experiencing how mother lets ME rest, teaches ME how to avoid pushing others too hard. ME learns to be respectful and not overwhelm others with my feelings.

I have noticed that the ability to handle *overwhelmed* is a sort of dividing line between people. There are those who will do anything to avoid getting overwhelmed. When they get overwhelmed, they collapse and don't know what to do. Others view being overwhelmed the way they would react to feeling cold or hungry. Certainly the feeling isn't desirable, but it can be endured for important causes. They continue to act like themselves even when overwhelmed. In the end they will not be daunted by any mountain or storm. St. Paul talks about being overwhelmed on his trips and perils—and yet he packed enough joy to continue his mission.

All of us know people who don't know when to stop. This comes paired with trouble regulating their own feelings (acting like themselves when they are upset). They certainly don't get back to joy very easily.

---

[1] Schore, Affect Regulations and the Origin of the Self page 424.

Why didn't they learn how to deal with overwhelmed feelings while climbing Mt. Joy? Their parents did not back off when they reached "overwhelmed." Instead of rest and a return to joy, their control center desynchronized and they learned to "lose it." This often happens when parents needed the child to be happy so the parents look and feel good or when parents are simply not available.

Hearing and joy
The second year of life is also devoted almost entirely to joy but with some important differences. By their first birthdays, their hearing has developed enough for babies to process sounds for meaning. While babies don't know what most words mean, babies can "read" voice-tone. They can tell when the voice is warm and joyful. For the second year of their lives, voice-tone becomes as important as the sight of a joyful face for reaching joy. A joyful voice-tone reaches around corners where eyes cannot. When babies can't see their parent's face they can hear the delight in a voice.

Singing is one of the leading sources of auditory joy. Fathers, mothers and families sing to their babies and bring joy. In time, singing becomes a major way for children to reach joy on their own.

Summary of Development, Attachment and the Senses[1]

0 - 1.5 months	Taste, smell and temperature
1.5 - 2.5 months	Touch
2.5 - 12 months	Visual (facial emotion)
12 - 24 months	Auditory (voice tone)

Each of these bonding senses supersedes the ones before by becoming dominant. Later modes of bonding add to, but do not eliminate, the earlier ones. Whichever mode is dominant works by receiving input that helps the baby's feelings move toward joy and euphoria. Infants bond to whoever provides this joy-effect, and they become like the joy source so that babies can create joy themselves after that.

By age two a baby's emotional thermostat is well on the way to being set. What the baby's body has felt for these months becomes the "normal" state the brain will seek for the rest of life. If this thermostat has been set to Joy Camp, joy will feel normal. If normal has been set as anxiety with an adrenaline buzz, that state will become normal. Every

---

[1] Schore, Affect Dysregulation and Disorders of the Self, pp 150-161

time we awaken our brain will try to restore "normal" for us. The same happens at bedtime. If normal is an anxious state, we will begin and end our days with worries. Blessedly, while many of us have had our normal set to depression, anxiety, anger, sadness and anything but Joy Camp, our brain can be retrained to Joy Camp later in life. Retraining doesn't happen automatically. We will explore how to retrain our normal in chapter three.

Importance of joy to God

Why dedicate two whole years to building joy into a child? As a culture, we overlook the importance of growing joy—out of ignorance. Some people have trouble believing that joy can be this important. Most of us are simply amazed by how early in life the strengths built on joy develop. But if building strength for a lifetime isn't reason enough, the place of joy in God's kingdom makes joy an eternal-life issue. The Psalmist says, "In thy presence is fullness of joy." (Psalms 16:10b KJV) God lives at the top of Mt. Joy—an excellent reason to help babies get there.

Jesus gave joy as the reason for his teaching. "These things have I spoken unto you, that my joy might remain in you, and that your joy might be full." (John 15:11 KJV) Jesus was training mountaineers.

The source of joy is attributed to God's face in a scripture that occurs in both the Old and New Testaments. This important text is part of the first public announcement of the good news of the Kingdom at Pentecost. Peter quotes from the Psalmist, "Thou hast made known to me the ways of life; thou shalt make me full of joy with thy countenance." (Acts 2:28 KJV) God's face fills us with joy just as the delighted parent's face fills a baby with joy.

Another psalm lists both sources of joy (auditory and visual.) "Blessed is the people that know the joyful sound: they shall walk, O LORD, in the light of thy countenance." (Psalms 89:15 KJV) God fills us with joy with joyful sounds and a face (His face) that lights up to see us. This blessing gives us strength. We should do the same for our children.

Chapter Three
One Year Old Me

I will turn their mourning into joy, and will comfort them, and make them rejoice from their sorrow. Jeremiah 31:13 KJV

About their first birthday our hardy little hikers can reliably reach the top of Joy Mountain. This strength will be put to use during the second year of their lives. During this year their mothers will teach them how to return to joy from all the unpleasant feelings in life. When a ME has a secure bond with someone who will help ME feel better after a painful emotion, the infant will grow strong and face hardship with hope.

FINDING THE WAY BACK TO JOY CAMP

Anyone who has taken young children camping knows how carefully they must be watched to be sure they don't wander off and get lost. When children learn how to get down off the rocks safely, find their way back from the hill on their own, and get back out of the woods without getting lost, parents heave a huge sigh of relief. Their child can now find camp from anywhere around. Camping becomes safer and far more fun.

In the same way, infants must learn the path back to Joy Camp from all their other feelings. They must be guided from shame back to joy, as well as from disgust, fear, sadness, disappointment, anger, hopelessness and humiliation. Once infants know the path back, they will not be intimidated or deterred by feelings. Another way to say this is that the baby can now quiet his own brain and feelings when emotions are in an uproar. She has learned to control her quieting circuits, not just when she must quiet her joy but when she must quiet her distress. Building joy is how ME developed these circuits and learned to control them.

Babies will only have as much strength to climb back to joy as they developed by climbing up Mt. Joy. If the sad feeling intensity, for instance, is higher than ME learned to climb on Mt. Joy, ME will run out of strength before getting back to Joy Camp. From then on ME will avoid that feeling instead of overcoming it. The control center in that brain does not have enough capacity or "bandwidth" and becomes desynchronized when the distressing emotion becomes too strong. The brain switches from goal directed actions to "help me" and then "make it stop."

Infants must be guided safely into these demanding feelings and back by their parents. The emotion on the mother's face or in her voice is the stimulus that takes the child "out into the woods." Let's say baby sticks his hand in his diaper. He is sure that Mommy will be glad to see him and see what he has done. Instead, Mommy suddenly shows disgust on her face. His brain copies the feeling and just as suddenly he is feeling disgusted and ashamed instead of joyful. Mommy then leads him back to joy by cleaning him up and then climbing Mt. Joy again together. "There! You smell better now!" she says with a smile.

For this to succeed it is necessary for two things to happen. The parent must share the "bad" feeling with the child and then return to a sense of connection together. The child's brain exactly mimics the parent's path back to joy. This shows the baby how to feel the feeling, quiet the feeling, stay relational, and be flexible at the same time. Baby experiences mutual mind during emotions creating a "return to joy map" and storing it in the right hemisphere of the brain.

Sadly, if the parent does not share the feeling and return to relational joy the child learns that also. Baby will conclude that there is no way back to relationships from that "bad" spot. If this loss happens frequently for certain emotions, the baby will lose hope. Instead of mutual repair of relationships the child will manage "bad" feelings in non-relational ways. What this means is that the child now lacks an element of social intelligence. This baby cannot use unpleasant emotional outcomes to improve relationships – at least for the feelings the infant now avoids.

The brain learns that no one will help and soon begins predicting that emotions mean no one will be on my side. Now the brain enters a sort of "enemy mode"[1] rather than the normal "relational mode" and people begin to feel like enemies to be stopped rather than loving relationships to be restored.

There are six emotional warning signals wired into the brain that signal six threats to relational joy. When an emotional alarm sounds we

---

[1] Wilder and Woolridge, Escaping Enemy Mode, (Chicago: Northfield, 2022).

lose our relational joy and enter into an "error condition" that must be corrected. Resilience depends on rapid repairs. These six joy interrupters come in the form of unpleasant emotions that signal a relational injury. These six alarm signals are:
1. Sadness = I am losing a source of joy
2. Fear = there is a threat we must escape
3. Anger = there is a threat we must stop
4. Shame = I am not bringing you joy right now
5. Disgust = something here is not life-giving
6. Hopelessness = I don't have the resources for this

By seeing the same feeling he is having expressed on Mommy's face the baby can duplicate her emotions, and even brain chemistry, each step of the way back to joy and quiet together. This is the map ME will use to find the way back to joy for the rest of life. Every time he is overwhelmed his brain will switch on the guidance images in his right brain—but pity the child who has none. Keep in mind that at this age babies have a vocabulary of only one or two words so they learn by imitation.

Hope is grown by linking minds with the baby while she is still in her terrible feeling. The mature parent begins sharing the baby's feeling before she gives up hope that she will find someone to show her the way back to joy. If the parent will not share the baby's feeling, baby has no one to mimic and learn her or his way back.

Because the fast track in the right brain reads and responds to emotional cues faster than conscious thought, the emotions and energy levels of the right brain can quickly be duplicated between two brains. Thus the fast tracks in both parent and baby brains can create a mutual-mind state between them. In this matched state the two brains develop the same chemistry, run the same circuits and reach the same result. The bigger brain leads the way.

A year of practice with joy has taught the baby brain to match the developed brain behind the face that baby loves. A well trained bigger brain can easily feel upset and still love. The baby brain cannot do both at first. Now by following this bigger mind, baby learns to use unpleasant emotions to create better relationships! That is, provided the bigger brain has learned how.

A rapid return to relationship is critical. Babies cry because they have hope that someone will find them and bring them back to joy. The parent must not exceed their baby's strength but rather comfort and restore joy before the baby's hope is gone. When we destroy a baby's capacity to hope it may well be destroyed for life. Proverbs reminds us that, "Hope deferred [or delayed] maketh the heart sick: but when the desire cometh, it is a tree of life." (Proverbs 13:12 KJV)

Healthy shame – say what?

Of all the unpleasant feelings perhaps shame is the most important one to recover from easily. Shame is a major component of all social interactions because shame is what we feel when others are not happy with us. Naturally, in the course of social learning, we will do many things that make others unhappy with us. The child who can return to joy and quiet feelings of shame will be a fast social learner. The child who cannot quiet shame will either be a social pleaser or demand to be pleased. This condition, known as narcissism[1] is a pain to be around. Children who can quiet shame and stay relational will be miles ahead in social intelligence.

What is healthy shame? Healthy messages remind us who we really are. Becoming ME rather than some strangely distorted **ME** depends entirely upon receiving healthy reminders when we forget our best selves. If we remember that the adult brain is one-third "be-like" stuff that will copy almost anything it becomes clear that we can easily copy something that is not good for us. We have all watched children pick up the wrong example through abuse or imitating a bad example. A healthy shame message says, "We are not like that" and then adds, "we are like this."

What is toxic shame? For simplicity we will say that toxic shame comes from a failure to offer a way to restore relational joy by being our true selves. One way this happens is when shame messages only tell us what is wrong and not what is right. Unrealistic messages about our true selves also produce toxic shame. The worst of these toxic shame messages occur when we are told that we are the "bad" rather than we need to learn the "good." Toxic shame develops when there is no one to share the shame with us on the way back to relational joy.

A healthy shame message looks like an encouragement to become my best ME. I might hear, "We don't hit our sisters when we want a toy. We are kind and use our words to ask nicely." A toxic shame message might sound like, "You bad boy! How many times have I told you not to hit!" Even without the "bad boy" comment the statement is still toxic

---

[1] See my book The Pandora Problem, (Carmel, IN: Deeper Walk International 2018) for a community solution to narcissism.

because 1) it does not tell how to be my best self or 2) give me any indication that someone will love me while I learn.

If babies were simply balloons that we inflate with good things until they are inflated we would not need healthy shame messages. But babies are made by copying others and babies will copy all sorts of things. We need ways to help them shed the incorrect or defective copies. Much like learning a language, we need to know when we copied the wrong sound, didn't form the sound correctly and what the proper sound is like.

There is a tendency in pop psychology to think we should avoid shame and only give positive messages. Positivity without the slight and momentary pain of shame does not let the brain register that change is needed. People who lose the ability to feel pain continue to injure themselves and do not learn from damaging experiences. A bit of shame pain helps learning but must be replaced with joy in less than ninety seconds to avoid toxicity.

Without learning how to use shame to improve relationships all shame will feel toxic to the relationally untrained brain. Because so many people no longer know how to use shame in healthy relational ways they react to every correction as though it were toxic.

Because shame is a "pain" signal to the brain that something has gone wrong in a relationship we quickly dislike anyone who deliberately causes us shame and leaves us there. When we are left in shame the brain moves quickly into enemy mode. Once in enemy mode we will feel attacked rather than corrected. We see people who might be helping us find ME as attackers and enemies rather than allies. What we need is help staying relational and becoming our best ME.

With practice the baby will find paths back to Joy Camp from everywhere and every difficult and draining feeling. The strength to feel feelings that the baby developed climbing Joy Mountain is combined with the path back to joy which builds: hope, resilience, confidence and a lack of self-centeredness. This last one may surprise you, but self-centeredness comes from avoiding anything that gives ME a bad feeling. Children that must avoid feelings spend far more time and effort on their self-interests. Conversely, a strong hope that disappointment will eventually reveal a path back to joy lets children take risks and think of others.

Consistently returning to joy after a hard feeling also makes one less self-centered because it teaches that satisfaction is reached when everyone is back in Joy Camp. Satisfaction comes from shared joy—not just finishing a job.

Remediating return to joy

Not only do mothers help children back to joy but good friends and counselors help people return to joy as well. When people have been poorly equipped to return to joy, their remedial relationships can help them find joy and then find the way back from the six relational warning feelings. Joy in this context means that I am not alone. Joy is a mutual mind state with someone who cares. Someone who is willing to be with me, share my feeling, show me how to control it by handling it themselves and still acting like a relational, loving person. This learning, like that with mother, is rapid and nonverbal, using facial expressions, voice tone, and body-cues from one right-hemisphere prefrontal cortex to the other.

Once a path back to relational joy has been established from each of these overwhelming feelings it is possible to make them a part of one's self and history. Now we can feel these feelings and still act like ourselves. Our brain's control center now stays synchronized during emotional signals. Without this way back to joy, people live in terror of their feelings and spend much of their energy avoiding anything that will set off the feelings leaving them out of control and miserable again.

Extremely strong emotional events can become traumas when we cannot return to joy from that emotion and we lack the joy strength to handle the intensity. Traumas cannot be faced or resolved in any helpful way until there is sufficient joy strength present to handle the intensity of every disorganizing feeling caused by the trauma. This means that a mature guide is needed who can share every intense feeling that desynchronized the traumatized person's brain. Counselors must know who they are in the presence of intense feeling, act like themselves, regulate their own emotions and help the traumatized person with theirs as well.

Jesus was a clear example of one who could face life unselfishly because he knew the way back to joy. In the quote that began chapter two Jesus indicated that joy brought women out of the distress of childbirth. Joy also brought Jesus through his hardest hour. "Who for the joy that was set before him endured the cross, despising the shame." (Hebrews 12:2 KJV.) He knew there was a path back from pain and shame. Returning to joy was how he approached his death. Many people have experienced Jesus as their guide out of trauma through mutual mind with him. Immanuel Prayer is one such experience.[1]

We should not even need to say it, but there are those who teach that Jesus endured the cross for a different reason. They teach that Jesus stayed on the cross because God did not come when he cried and therefore, we also should not come when our children cry! Let me say it again, Jesus was motivated by his desire to return to joy. Babies do not have this capacity! His hope and joy was greater than the pain or the great distress he felt—and it takes a lot of joy to do that. He could stay on course because he knew the path back to Joy Camp. Babies develop this strength each time their parents comfort them as they cry.

"My God, my God, why have you forsaken me?" is the loud cry that Jesus uttered on the cross. It has been cited as proof that God did not comfort Jesus on the cross, but this is not true. As he often does, Jesus is singing—in this case Psalm 22, the song that begins with just these words. The psalm is a song and anyone who knew it would have recognized the opening line just as we would know *Amazing Grace*. Read the whole Psalm but notice the following verses:

1a	My God, my God, why have you forsaken me?
4a	In you our fathers put their trust;
5	They cried to you and were saved; in you they trusted and were not disappointed.
9-11	Yet you brought me out of the womb; you made me trust you even at my mother's breast. From birth I was cast upon you; from my mother's womb you have been my God. **Do not be far from me**, for trouble is near and there is no one to help.
19	But you, O Lord, **be not far off**; O my Strength **come quickly** to help me.
24	For he has not despised or disdained the suffering of the afflicted one; he has not hidden his face from him but listened to his cry for help. (NIV emphasis mine)

This is an anthem to a trust that was built from birth with assurance that comfort and help were never far away. Even in suffering there was face-to-face contact that quickly brought strength. What a song!

Jesus' next recorded words, and the last words before he died, were also a song. "Into thy hands I commit my spirit," comes from Psalm 31. Songs help us stay synchronized. Since our brain's control center is our

---

[1] Passing the Peace by Life Model Works. See also https://www.immanuelapproach.com/

center for synchronization, it is little wonder that the control center responds to songs and poetry but not to prose. Singing, even singing to ourselves, helps us stay synchronized in our distress.

There are many scriptures that will tell us that we can return to joy from times of distress.

- Weeping may endure for a night, but joy cometh in the morning. (Psalms 30:5 KJV)
- They that sow in tears shall reap in joy. (Psalms 126:5 KJV)
- [From] their shame...and confusion...they shall rejoice. (Isaiah 61:7 KJV)
- I will turn their mourning into joy, and will comfort them, and make them rejoice from their sorrow. (Jeremiah 31:13 KJV)
- Make me to hear joy and gladness; that the bones which thou hast broken may rejoice. (Psalms 51:8 KJV)

Many of these scriptures come from the psalms or songs of God. Singing our way to joy is strongly recommended. Many of the Psalms start a long way from joy and then we follow as the psalmist sings us back home to Joy Camp.

It was Christmas day, the year I was two, that my first real return to joy test arrived. I suffered a stroke during Christmas dinner that paralyzed half my body. In an hour I was in the grip of a raging fever, ultimately diagnosed as viral meningitis. Whenever the fever would lift for a moment, I would pull myself up the bars of my crib and sing "Hosanna to the King of Kings" with all my strength. I was singing myself back to joy—a practice I still continue.

Finding the path back from every feeling starts at age one and takes a year to practice. Four months into this practice the limbic system matures. The limbic system amplifies the intensity of all the baby's emotions. When the system kicks in at sixteen months of age, instead of anger we get rage and tantrums. Instead of fear we get terror and night terrors. For the baby whose brain knows the way back to joy, this is just a harder workout. But for those whose feelings have no path back to Joy Camp, there is terrible suffering.

Two months later, at eighteen months of age, the brain attempts to unify our emotional identity into one solid ME. The plan is to connect all the separate emotional areas within a ring of joy. Perhaps this structure in the brain does not look much like a ring but it functions like one.

THE RING OF JOY

Until a year and a half old, babies handle each emotion separately, as though they were different people for each emotion. Each feeling has its own brain center that works independently. This is part of why good mothering teaches babies how to return to joy from each feeling. These emotional centers are located around the bottom of the brain. At eighteen months the joyful identity region (rPFC) attempts to grow a control network that connects all of these emotional centers together. This "ring" around the bottom of the brain establishes, for the first time, that the baby is the same person no matter what he or she feels. In time this ring of joy will allow me to act like ME regardless of the feeling.

Keep in mind that as the ring forms a baby's expressive vocabulary is only about fifteen words. Baby's sense of identity comes from memories of a responsive face that is present no matter what ME feels. If ME has worked out on Mt. Joy and found ways back from each feeling, ME will now grow a strong, united self. If not, the distress caused by this failure to return to joy will become stress and release the stress hormone— cortisol. Cortisol will burn out any weak connections and newly formed connections in the brain isolating those emotional centers even further. Without training, these feeling centers will stay disconnected acting like separate selves. These separated regions will always produce a desynchronization of ME—the brain's emotional control center when they are triggered. In the future people will say that I am "moody" or change when I get angry or frightened—whatever the disconnected feelings might be. An incomplete or weak ring of joy is an invitation for psychological problems like identity splitting, addictions, mood swings, dissociation and behavior problems.

The main effect of childhood trauma and deprivation is the inability to regulate feelings.[1] In other words, people are not able to act like themselves, maintain a consistent ME or return to joy once they have a strong unpleasant feeling. They do not know how to be like themselves when they are upset. We mentioned earlier that brain activity studies indicate an underdeveloped identity structure in these individuals who can't regulate or recover from upset.[2]

---

[1] Schore, Affect Regulation and the Repair of the Self 2003, p. 141.
[2] Ibid pp. 235-6

Sometimes, incomplete formation of the ring produces a strange result. When there are paths back to joy from some feelings but not others, the person will learn to move from a "no path back" emotion to one that "has a path." If a man has no path back to joy from anger then whenever he gets angry (no path back) he goes to hurt and sad (path back.) A different man who has a path back to joy from anger will go from shame or hopeless despair (with no paths back to joy) to angry (path back) and start a fight because he learned that sometimes after fights people kiss and make up.

A strong joy ring will help people act like themselves (stay ME) whether they are frightened, angry, sad, hurt or happy. Again Jesus gives us an example. When he was sad he healed, the same when he was tired, we are even told that once he got so angry he healed a man (Mark 3:5.) Jesus always acted like himself. That is why he creates in us the ability to grow joy rings. We are creatures of joy.

Setting and Resetting Normal
As the brain is setting up one single ME identity with many different feelings needed for good relationships it is also establishing its "normal." Nerve cells burn a lot of energy so setting normal saves energy. The way the infant has felt most often for the first eighteen months establishes normal. If the family was depressed from a death or illness, or parents were anxious due to lack of money or war or if their personalities tended to be angry – all these factors contributed to a sense of normal.

Before we can hardly talk our brain sets environmental feelings as the "normal" for our lives. From then on, the brain tries to reset to normal when we awaken or go to sleep or if something unusual happens. Do we wake up feeling anxious? Do pleasant experiences drift away quickly? Our brain is working hard to kept things "normal."

Later in life we may struggle against our angry, worried, depressed or unloved sense of normal but our brain quickly finds its way back to miserable each morning or after anything positive happens. We begin to believe that good things don't last and that miserable can be expected again tomorrow. Without retraining our brain to a new normal that is exactly what will happen.

We want joy as our new normal but joy is relational. Do you remember that it took eighteen months to set normal? As adults we cannot find people to smile at us up to eight hours a day for months. Instead, we need a work-around.

The feeling our brains experience after joyful interactions is appreciation. We can trigger appreciation almost any time through experiences and memories. Appreciation is a body memory.

The first step to a new normal is learning to feel appreciation in my body on-demand. Appreciation, gratitude or thankfulness do their work as long as I notice what appreciation/thankfulness feels like in my body. Noticing my body's feelings insures that the right parts of my brain are working together (prefrontal cortex, anterior cingulate and insula.) When my brain discovers that I can feel appreciation whenever I try, a new range of positive possibilities opens for ME.

The second step toward a new normal is learning to sustain the feeling of appreciation for five straight minutes. To do this I collect a series of appreciation experiences and memories to string together. By giving each appreciation experience a name, ME can jump from one to the next and keep appreciation going. Names could be: island sunrise, morning coffee, Fido at the lake or Julie's birthday. Now ME can keep my appreciation going longer by remembering one appreciation experience after another. When ME can do this for five minutes my brain realizes that I can feel good as long as I like.

The third step to a new normal positions my positive appreciation experiences strategically across my day. Starting and ending my day with appreciation and throwing in a dose in the middle helps my brain realize, "I can do this all day." By practicing five minutes of appreciation three times a day for a month ME has a chance to reset normal. The brain is a learning machine. Once it knows how to feel good, keep that good feeling going and experience a good feeling any time of day it decides, "I'll make this my new normal!"

Practice, Practice and More Practice
The six month period from eighteen to twenty four months is spent growing a strong unified ME. Many trips back to joy from all sorts of feelings establish the first large-scale integration of identity. This also allows a baby to realize that mother is the same person whether she is angry or joyful with the baby. All paths lead to joy.

If we have ever started a business or office from scratch we can imagine the challenge the baby's brain faces in organizing itself into a personality. Establishing a unified ME has not been easy. Our baby has spent the first half of infancy getting their personality established and synchronized. They did it by finding out who was paying attention to them and seeking mutual control of their emotions (through their faces) long enough experience relational joy. Infancy is the only time when a human being's ME can actually be controlled by another person. Through these mutual experience the baby has learned to be-like mother, or whoever was closest. This window closes as infants pass their second birthday. The relational side of ME is now in place and running the brain's fast track.

Chapter Four
Infants from Two to Four

But if you bite and devour one another, take care that you are not consumed by one another.   Galatians 5:15 NASV

On their second birthday infants are one half the height they will be when full grown. Baby can walk, talk and self-regulate feelings when things go wrong. Almost daily our baby discovers he or she can do something he couldn't the day before. During this time of left hemisphere growth she learns thoughtful skills for self-care, self-expression, and self-regulation. The next two years will be devoted to discovering what I can do.[1] "I can do it myself!" is the theme.

Children seem ready to climb on anything. Part of safety is navigating physical hazards. They don't understand the limits of their capacities and will get into dangers they cannot handle. Infants will put harmful things in their mouths. All human babies are born as predators. Putting everything that they can reach into their mouths is innate. For babies, the world is mine to eat. Mommy goes in my mouth and exists to feed me. Everything and everyone is my food. I can be totally upset if I can't eat what I want.

THE SECOND HALF OF INFANCY

During the first half of infancy the mother has an advantage over the average father. She guesses more easily what baby feels and needs, helps him reach joy, leads him out of Joy Camp and back again. A father is not usually as gifted at these things but during the second half of infancy he has the advantage. Human parents divide baby training demands because it difficult for the one who has been protecting baby from all harm to switch to teaching "my baby" to take risks and face threats. The second half of infancy involves moving out of safety into

---

[1] Erik Erikson's autonomy stage. www.simplypsychology.org/erik-erikson.html

taking risks. Safety now depends upon understanding the threats and risks. We are talking about the balance between risk taking and safety.

As baby reaches two and begins exploring the world it becomes important to face risks and learn safety. Dads seem to be first to throw babies in the air and swing them around. Dads seem to have the gift of believing their baby's can "do it."

There is some brain basis for the gender differences associated with this selective specialization. Some *potentially* protective systems are stronger in the male brain and, if father knows how, he becomes the best baby trainer. If a father intuitively knows how to protect, the baby's training begins about eighteen months of age and develops a significant attachment between baby and dad. If dad learned to a) handle his emotional energy safely and b) developed his protector skills, this adventure will go well.

Human communities have tended to specialize brain training by gender but not without incurring some risks. The active question is whether the father is going to train the child to be a protector or a more effective predator. Traditional roles have included both kinds of training. Thinking like predators also helps men hunt the same large game as other apex predators.

People who learn to think like predators will be more effective as either predators or protectors. Understanding vulnerabilities lets people either exploit or protect using that knowledge. Hiring "hackers" by cybersecurity firms is one example of this tension.

Most predators will attack their own species at times. Lions, one of the predators that people have watched and emulated for a long time, are one example. While female lions hunt for most of the food, male lions fight other males and then kill all the cubs of the defeated lion. The winner then has his own cubs with all the lionesses.

Predators present a large risk to infants of every species. Predators often target mothers with infants. The more predators there are in the environment the harder it will be for mothers and babies to get around safely. Human skill development has been selectively shaped by predator threats and some patterns have been internalized. In human communities, the main predators who put women and children at risk are human.[1]

---

[1] It would be interesting to know what trends may have developed on islands where, for many generations, people have been the only land predator. But, that is not in my life experience.

Becoming protectors

Now, no one is taking our two-year-old out to chase lions so you may be wondering why introduce the predator problem now? In my preface to this 2024 edition I mentioned that men have contributed disproportionately to the inhumanity in the human communities I have seen. The men who have caused the damage were most often active predators. The predatory systems in the brain are larger in males and need careful training to become protective. That training is already starting the second half of infancy. The outcome of this training in males, who need a bit more training than females, heavily impacts future generations.

In healthy families, when babies turn one their mothers start training them to stay relational with shame and the other five unpleasant emotions. By age two a well trained ring of joyful identity now stays relational during all six unpleasant emotions by quieting itself.

At about eighteen months the intelligent branch of the autonomic nervous system (that regulates predatory behavior and high energy emotional energy states) matures enough to train. Dad is now in line to train the predatory system to stay relational. The key protective element involves learning to control the highly emotional energy states in which people often damage one another.

Play is how infants, and later children, learn to control their high energy states. The training for protection in the presence of threats is learned by what we might call "rough play." Rough play takes the baby to the edge of danger (harm), stops a second and then repeats. The "trainer" must be tuned into the vulnerabilities and weaknesses of the baby and stop protectively every time the limits are near – but not yet reached. Hundreds and thousands of cycles teaches the baby to know safe limits and stop in time to prevent injury. If not, someone gets hurt.

Learning when to stop[1] is learned best with father about ages sixteen to thirty-six months. There are a wide variety of predator stopping games that fathers can play. At one end are tickling games and at the other are the "I'm coming to get you" games. These games delight children if and only if the adult knows when to stop. Games turn into torture and torment when the adult does not know when to stop. The mock predator stalks the victim as the excitement builds but stops and rests at the first sign of "that is too much." Knowing when to stop is

---

[1] Coursey, Transforming Fellowship: 19 Brain Skills that Build Community, (East Peoria, IL: Shepherd's House, 2016).

learned by children through hundreds of these cycles and eliminates predatory excesses later in life. Stopping in time teaches compassion. Learning when to stop develops a major social skill needed for good relationships between adults as much as between adults and children.

Most people are shocked both by how early this training begins and who should do it. We carefully develop early reading but carelessly leave predatory, emotional and relational training to chance. Baby, meanwhile, is a copy machine who is learning predatory examples from other children, adults and media. Instead of learning to be protective, many learn to be effective predators during anger, desires and other impulses as they get older.

Predatory brain systems track weakness and use it to advantage. No one has to teach a child to notice weakness. Children notice and will often point out any defect or weakness in others without needing special instruction. When predator systems are in charge, children notice the pain of others but do not share that pain. We often see this expressed as a cold anger. As people get older this lack of shared pain becomes the way they deal with enemies.

Dad has larger brain system for dealing with predatory behavior and cold anger. If baby is to learn to be protective and compassionate the best model comes from how Dad has mastered his own "enemy mode."[1] But, has he? For that matter, has Mom? The risk of predatory responses is not just a male problem. Women seeking power (often because it has been taken from them) also risk staying predatory. Does anger turn people into enemies at home? Do parents exploit each other's weaknesses?

Enemy mode sounds like a strong term for something that happens frequently in every family. But, we can easily feel that the people close to us are not on our side. We all have moments when we don't really care what others feel and we want to win. We all take advantage of weak moments when others will not be watching to get a toy, treat or forbidden access. Children know exactly which parent to ask for something they want and when to ask. Children know just what one parent does not tell the other. These are all the brain's enemy mode in action – a stealthy predatory activity that we dress up socially as best we can.

Fights and divorces, cheating, hidden porn habits and all sexual exploitation employ enemy mode patterns. Relationships become

---

[1] Wilder and Woodridge, *Escaping Enemy Mode: How our brains unite or divide us*, (Chicago: Northfield, 2022).

conquests, business becomes a place to win and people's weaknesses a way to get ahead. Whenever we see manipulation, deception, hate, coldness and a lack of compassion we are watching the brain's enemy mode. Some people will live their whole life in this predatory pattern.[1]

If our brain cannot deal with any one of the six unpleasant emotions in a relational way it goes into enemy mode. When little two year old predators are angry because they don't get what they want, it is time to train them to stay relational – even while others feel like enemies to them. Learning how to stay relational is what a two year old needs to learn from parents with Dad as the main trail guide. This is technical climbing and made possible by a strong relational joy bonds.

Working

From two to four the baby's identity is focused on what he can do. In some cultures children are helpful, work at home with pride and without complaining. These children begin helping when they are about two years old. Even at two, children want to be important and have something to contribute to their families. Having something to give also reduces sibling rivalry. Rather than competing for what parents can give them, two-year-olds enjoy seeing what they can give to family members. Paying and rewarding two-year-olds for work actually decreases their satisfaction and desire to work. Working at home and having something to give is a game changer at this age. If we wait until babies lose interest in working with the family then getting their help when they are teenagers will be like pulling teeth.

Using words

The first half of infancy was the growth spurt for the right hemisphere portion of the identity structure of the prefrontal cortex. The left half of our be-like stuff makes us people of words and language. This verbal region lets us think in words about who we are. Once again we will become like the people around us in our speech. Words are here to stay.

The second half of infancy is when the left hemisphere prefrontal region grows to become one sixth of the adult brain. Understanding the left brain is quite a bit easier for us because it runs slowly. At conscious speed we can sense and watch what is happening in our minds. We can notice ourselves looking for words, trying to explain and focusing on a subject.

---

[1] Wilder, The Pandora Problem, (Carmel: Deeper Walk Publishing, 2018) has more on learning our way out of enemy mode as adults.

Our conscious slow track specializes in focused problem solving. This ability to focus and problem solve prevents the left brain from ever seeing the whole picture. Therefore, our words, explanations and conscious awareness are always a bit "tunnel visioned" and limited. None the less, our conscious identity, language and ideas are also ways we learn to be ME.

As we learn language, several problems can develop if parents are not aware of exactly how their child understands words. All too frequently parents increase their conflict with two-year-olds with a simple *parent error*. "I told him not to do it and he looked right at me, defied me and did it!" is a common complaint by parents. This is *parent error*! Let's see why.

When they are first learning language children's brains cannot grasp a negative command. For some children this continues until they reach five years of age. This is particularly true for children under pressure or emotion. At first:

"Don't hit your sister!" means the same as "Hit your sister!"

"Don't touch it!" is heard as "Touch it!"

"Don't leave the yard!" equals "Leave the yard!"

Our brains understand negative statements as positive commands with a stop sign at the end, so we stop. The capacity to add stop signs develops as late as age five. Until then, children can hear the words just fine but they can't reliably interpret the meaning. If I told you to "Stop misatuning!" you might have this sort of problem in reverse. You could understand that you were to stop—but stop what? Children under five understand the "what" but not the "stop." They hear:

"(mumble) hit your sister!"

"(something or another) touch it!"

"(unintelligible) leave the yard!"

As a result two-year-olds will look at their parents to see if they are serious! "Hit my sister? Are you kidding? That gets me in trouble! Oh my though, mother looks serious." And so the dirty deed is done.

This problem is made worse for children who become confused at age two and stop listening to words. Before long the infant is so confused that they will go back to using the non-verbal right hemisphere and decide what to do by voice-tone. Soon his parents will be saying, "She never obeys until I have to yell at her!" *Parent error* again! The child is sorting out commands by voice-tone because if she obeys them all (both the negative and positive which she cannot yet sort out) she will get punished. This leads children to believe their parents are not fair, lie and torment them. It generates lots of anger for the child who gets punished or scolded for doing what he understood he was told to do. Adding anger to a two-year-old gives bad results.

To correct this problem, stay in tune with your child's language development. All the important commands given to children under five should be positive. If you have trouble making positive commands out of negative ones it will help you understand the impossibility this poses for the two-year-old mind. Negative commands must be translated by the parent's brain into useful instructions the child can follow. For instance:

"Don't hit your brother!" becomes "Play nicely with your brother!"
"Don't touch it!" becomes "Keep your hands down and look!"
"Don't leave the yard!" becomes "Stay in the yard!"

Once these parent errors are eliminated, living with two-year-olds is smoother and at times even exciting. Still, when two-year-olds get upset, everything stops until they feel better. Whenever they find themselves having "bad" feelings, thinking and exploring stop. The control center in their right hemisphere takes over. All of their joyful identity and the maps back to joy should be stored there by now. They abandon the left side of the brain with all its words and thoughts while switching on the "return to joy" map on the right side. They suddenly function like one-year-old babies in that words have no effect. This is how the brain is wired. Of course, if there is no map back to joy for this feeling the toddler will stay in her or his distress. Only after returning to joy will the two-year-old be back. At this age the two halves of the brain might just as well be sitting in different skulls.

Because of their reputation, many people give up too quickly on two-year-olds leaving them lost outside of Joy Camp. Don't call your two-year-old a baby when she gets upset. Help him find joy. Much of the stress we call the "terrible twos" comes from trying to control a child **before** returning her to joy. Remember that while he is upset his word processing left hemisphere is shut off and will only be back once joy is reached. First help her with her feeling then you can instruct her once again. Parents who make their control the number one issue at this age will not produce courageous children. Returning to joy is the number one priority, learning to obey is number two. These two tasks can only be combined next year—after the necessary brain connections grow at age three.

When it comes to maturity, sooner is not better. If you were exploring a road that was just being built and came to a river with a sign, "Bridge to be built next year," would you try to drive your family across the chasm? Let us respect the places where our creator has not yet built bridges in children's minds. Two-year-olds will only explore and discover while they feel joy. It keeps them out of some trouble they can't understand.

AGE THREE

Joining of the two hemispheres happens at age three. The connections that begin growing will help the verbal and feeling halves of the infant's identity to discover each other. In this last year of infancy toddlers can learn to put words and feelings together. For the first time they can talk about what they are doing, even when they feel upset. They begin learning how to act like themselves when they have a feeling. They learn what they want to do and say when things go wrong. This last year of infancy, actions and identity come together. No longer do they become one-year-olds when upset. Now, for the first time they can think about obeying even if they feel upset.

Parents still find themselves busy teaching three-year-olds how to control themselves using thoughts and words. Because the capacity to imagine is not yet fully developed for infants, they still do almost everything by imitation. Teaching them how to talk about themselves requires parental examples and a safe environment to explore, discover and grow. Parents set limits and encourage-encourage-encourage.

The impact of abuse
One researcher discovered that children who had been mistreated failed to develop their left hemispheres very well. Their mental energy was used trying to keep an emotional balance. There was little energy left for language learning or thinking about the world. This researcher found that, for infant boys in particular, neglect greatly damaged the development of the bridge between left and right hemispheres.[1] In boys, neglect produced worse damage than abuse.

Trauma and neglect may leave lasting deficits. We all know people who become one-year-olds when they get upset. They can think of nothing else but their feelings. Their right hemispheres take over and are not consulting with their left. Words don't help. The bridge is closed or

[1] Teicher, Martin H., Scars That Won't Heal: The Neurobiology of Child Abuse, Scientific American, March 2002.

out. While upset, they only notice voice-tone and can't go on until they feel better. Others may be obviously angry, sad or afraid but the talking/thinking half of their brain has not been notified at all. I can remember one man with tears running down his face who had no idea he was sad. He could not explain why there were tears when he spoke of his father's death. This is an extreme example of a common problem.

Long-term memory

About the time of our third birthday another amazing capacity develops. The brain begins storing long-term memories. With long term memories and a bridge between words and feelings, what we remember can change how we think. What we think can change the way we feel. We can remember things when we stop to try and we can talk about our experiences later. The equipment is all there but without training this capacity means nothing. Until now, all experiences and upsets had to be processed instantly and on the spot. With long-term memory the potential to take lessons with us or wait to work things through later give a huge increase in the baby's resilience and capacity. The year ahead until an infant's fourth birthday will be training and practice time. Once childhood exploration and self-care begins these skills need to be in place.

Seeing what God sees

Seeing what God sees is an essential skill to learn as long term memories form. We call this ability Godsight[1] or iSight[2] and it is a learned ability to recognize when God is helping us think. Grace – the understanding that we are special without doing anything to earn it – is the result of seeing babies as God sees them While it is the parents' responsibility to see babies through God's eyes[3] it is also the parents' privilege to teach babies how to see everyone through God's eyes. Godsight is easy to learn when joy is high. Godsight is helpful to have when the six unpleasant emotions are running. During infancy it is the parents' responsibility to see babies as God sees babies.

One element of Godsight that is very easily found in Jesus is compassion. Regardless of the situation, Jesus felt and showed compassion. One cannot know Jesus and fail to have compassion. One

[1] Coursey, Transforming Fellowship; also Coursey and Brown, Relational Skills in the Bible; and also THRIVE Training.
[2] iSight is short for "Immanuel Sight" (knowing God is with us). Joyful Journey is a great introductory text.
[3] Ed Khouri, Becoming a Face of Grace: Navigating lasting relationship with God and others, (Illumify 2021).

cannot see what God sees and not respond with compassion. We cannot love enemies or get out of enemy mode effectively without compassion. In fact, the difference between how enemy mode exploits weakness and relational mode protects weakness is simply compassion. Both enemy mode and relational mode see the weakness and know how it feels but only relational mode cares. Enemy mode uses weaknesses to win. It might not be a stretch to say the Christians should be learning to live their whole lives in relational mode. Jesus instructs us to love our enemies so we attach and care while others are still in enemy mode.

Growing compassion
While almost all children are able to notice weaknesses that cause pain to others there is a wide range of differences in how children respond. Some children easily share the pain of others while some children rarely do. These responses are a combination of natural traits and experiences that are shaped by social learning. While we fairly easily see pain in others what we do in response is largely learned. Do we respond with a relational compassion or a calculated enemy mode style? Significant people in a baby's life may model either option.

The last year of infancy is an important time to show young minds how to express compassion. During the child stage (age four to twelve) many children have their compassion damaged through school experiences. There is plenty of enemy mode and criticism flowing in most schools. Children can and will be cruel to each other. Adults with diminished compassion are not rare either. Parents without compassion are not rare. Seeing what God sees should be learned early.

Making shalom our normal
Shalom is a word for those moments when everything is right – the right amount of the right things in the right place at the right time for a totally settled experience. Living in shalom[1] is a major aspect of building compassion. Turbulent early years set a sense of normal that is anything but relationally peaceful. St. Paul suggests that the lack of this shalom should warn us that our relationships have gone wrong.[2] Shalom should be normal and alarms should sound if shalom is missing. Families need to teach this sense of normal to their babies. When we lose our shalom we need to stop and see what God sees to restore our individual and family shalom. Babies need to learn that this stopping and seeing what

[1] Passing the Peace by Life Model Works (lifemodelworks.org) is a good introductory booklet for learning to live in shalom as a family.
[2] Colossians 3:15

God sees is normal life and not some rare and remote religious experience. Knowing when to stop is a big part of life in shalom.

Mother's part in shalom needs more attention
The second half of infancy toddlers have learned all the lessons needed to take care of themselves. Soon the responsibility will be handed over to each child for self-care and self-expression. Having learned the basics about being human, infancy comes to an end. In four short years babies have copied the older minds around them and created working identities. In all likelihood, the mind they have copied most has been their mother's. This bond between mother and baby is one we must study further before we can leave infancy behind.

Chapter Five
Babies and Mothers

But Mary kept all these things and pondered them in her heart.
Luke 2:19 KJV

Our second son was born at home on the kitchen table. Before the cord was cut, our son had cried and started nursing at his mother's breast. His mother had wanted him to be born at home surrounded by family. Linda, our neighbor, was waiting downstairs to hear the news and started the phone calls as soon as the shout reached her through the back window, "It's a boy, Linda!" My wife just smiled and reached for the baby.

We had been to many classes and doctor's visits to prepare for childbirth at home. We watched movies and read books. We talked to doctors, nurses, midwives, mothers who had chosen home-births, and people from countries where children are usually born at home. Unlike all the preparation we needed for giving birth, our baby just did his work. He immediately began to breathe. Within two minutes of birth he had cried, expressing his needs, and received the milk and comfort he needed from his mother. Our baby was growing. To understand a baby's work we must look intimately at his or her needs from the infant's perspective. Meeting these needs will be the first order of business for the next twelve years.

MOTHER AND HER INFANT

Strange that the second thing our baby boy needed was to nurse at a breast. Men find it uncomfortable to think and talk about needs that way. A baby boy needs a breast. It will keep him alive, content, comforted, busy and connected to his world. To him it is love, acceptance, food, life, activity and warmth. It gives him something to smell, touch and see. A breast makes him feel better. The breast becomes a baby's first focus in the life-giving bond between him and his mother. I have intentionally focused on boys because men seem to have so many issues with breasts.

Take a few moments to imagine a baby boy's world. This new world is very unfamiliar, a place of sudden changes. In the midst of daily confusion there are the regular and relaxing workouts on Mother's breast. To a baby, this is warm life and dining satisfaction. The baby needs a connection to the breast. This connection brings life. From this connection he begins to understand all other connections in his or her life.

Soon baby will connect with Mommy's eyes as well, for her loving gaze will nurture his soul the way her breast has fed his body. For about the next three years, until he is weaned and ready to care for himself, she will largely be responsible for the quality of his life.

It is the nature of the bond between baby and mother that is crucial for development. Throughout this chapter we will talk about *mother* while keeping in mind that sometimes *mother* is not the one who gave birth to him. Sometimes *mother* is not even female.

Who is a mother? A story from the wise king Solomon answers this question. Two women were fighting over one baby. In that story, Solomon ordered a sword be brought to divide the contested baby in two. One woman said that would be fair, the second said it would be better to give the baby to her rival than to kill it. Solomon recognized the second woman's actions as motherly toward the baby and declared her the mother. You see, mothers find their babies' needs more important than their own feelings. So let's look at a baby's needs and mother's responses.

I will also continue to call baby "he" and mother "she" because it makes English so much easier to write and understand. This way the reader knows that "she" is mother and "he" is baby although in actual practice "mother" may not be a female and more than half the times "he" will be a girl baby.

The mother of a dependent, unweaned infant is truly a marvel of creation. This mother knows when he is sleepy, hungry or wet and when he needs attention and exploration. She is available, knows where he hurts (like when that new tooth is coming in), and keeps him the right temperature. Further, she thinks he is marvelous. Her eyes meet his greatest need, for to be fully alive he must be the sparkle in someone's eye. Mommy's gaze alone will bring him to unbearable levels of euphoria. His rapture is so deep, that the baby must look away to catch his breath.

The baby receives without knowing at first that he is asking or receiving. Mother knows his cry is asking. She knows turning his head toward her is asking. She knows that his tugging at her blouse is asking, so she teaches him by saying "Is my little baby hungry?" Sometimes he is not hungry for food but hungry for connection with her instead. He learns that he needs something and he learns to ask. He did not know that before.

It is with Mother's help that her baby will learn he has needs. Mother guesses these needs from his cries and actions. Her mind is specially designed for this moment and effort. Mommy guesses he is too hot or too cold, that he needs a nap or needs to be burped. Perhaps she guesses his cry means his tooth is coming in, and he needs something to chew. Most times he just needs her. Mother recognizes intuitively that his cries ask for something. From within the core of her motherhood come the words for his request. Slowly, and in time, her baby learns to use words to express his needs until one day they are expected from him. When that day comes, Mother will say, "How do you ask?" which means he forgot to say, "Please."

Mother is the first source of connection for a baby. From his connection with Mommy he learns many things: he learns to eat, sleep, to take in what is good and to cry for what he wants. She is his consumer's guide to all that is good and pleasing. With Mother's help and guesses, her baby learns how to find all the essential things he will ever need, such as: comfort, shelter, food, closeness, joy, rest and play. He also learns about his own body—where it begins and ends, its powers and limitations.

A good mother notices her baby's growth. She does not limit her focus to the things she gives him but notices what he can give. After keeping him safe, full, and warm she stops to enjoy what her baby can do. The good mother watches her baby grow and change. By watching what he does and how he contributes to the world, Mommy can appreciate his uniqueness. In time, he will learn to appreciate himself as well. But, for now, the infant does not know that he or she is unique.

A baby's mother shares her joy in him with others. Love is not threatened by such sharing. She knows that he needs more love than just her own. She knows that her own mind and skills are not complete and must be supplemented for her baby's best development. The good mother finds other mothers for her child, so that he may benefit from more care and attention than she can provide. Often these other mothers are female relatives, sometimes they are friends. Mommy fills his life with good people while he still does not know he needs them. Perhaps the main person that mother shares him with is his dad, but older siblings are very important as well. Together they explore and enjoy the uniqueness of her infant. He, in turn, learns that love is to be shared, not hoarded.

LOVE-BONDS AND FEAR-BONDS

Not all strong bonds between mother and child are good. In fact, bonds can be generally sorted into two types. Both types of bonds bring closeness between mother and child and serve to meet needs, but there the similarities end. Both fear and love can bond us to others. Fear or love can motivate our behavior. Fear or love can even produce similar behavior but they develop wildly different brain systems and patterns. But, in the case of a mother-and-baby bond, fear produces defective connections. Fear and love are antagonists to each other.

Love allows us to see the other person for who they are. Contrary to the popular expression, love is not blind. To mother a baby well, a mother must accurately sense her child's feelings and needs and put words and actions to them. Her child will then feel known, understood, and cared for. When the bond between mother and child is based on fear, his mother can no longer see her baby and his needs clearly. She wraps him in a blanket because she is afraid of what other mothers will think of her. She keeps him from exploring because she is afraid he will hurt himself. She feeds him because she is afraid he will get sick or grouchy. She hushes his crying because she fears others will think she is a bad mother. As a result, her baby will not know his needs or recognize his feelings. He learns his mother's fears instead. For such a baby, *life becomes a long-term effort to keep people from becoming upset or afraid.* He is controlled by his mother, even when he rebels, for rebellion is also fear.

GOOD AND BAD MOTHERING

The characteristics of a good mother are the emotional equivalents of a good musician: timing, intensity (volume) and tone. Did you ever take music lessons? I took piano lessons. You know, it wasn't easy to hit the right note at the right time and volume. Keeping everything synchronized was hard to learn. Babies come with fairly disorganized and undeveloped brains that must eventually be synchronized into happy kids that talk, smile, learn and are a joy to be around. You might say that the main function of good mothering is to teach her infant how to synchronize his brain inside and out. A quick look at how this is done will help us see the difference between good and bad mothering.

In every working human brain, a four-level control track on the right side of the brain dominates all of life. This control system runs faster than the conscious mind and maintains our identities as individuals, families and groups. Training this fast-track is accomplished through interactions with mother. Most of the training will be over by the end of the baby stage of life. One of the four levels of the control track, known also at the "mother core," will get special attention in this chapter because its early growth is heavily shaped through relationship with mother.

Like any part of our mind, the control center can learn a lot or end up ignorant and disorganized. When a mother's brain is ignorant and disorganized emotionally, she will train her baby the same way. When her mind has received good training she will pass on her learned abilities. This synchronization capacity is the main difference between good and bad mothering.

THE BRAIN'S CONTROL CENTER

You didn't know your brain had a control center? Our brains do some things we are aware of and other things we can't notice directly. We are more aware of our temperature than our blood pressure for example. Half of the control center is buried below our awareness. The first two layers of the control center are powerful influences but are located below the cortex. In the cortex we have a sense of self-awareness and will. The top two levels of the control center are cortical this giving us a chance for direct awareness of what they do.

The control center develops in the right brain. Control comes by maintaining our peace and relational joy through emotional regulation. A well trained fast-track allows a baby to regulate his own feelings, calm down and return to joy—provided he was taught how.

The right side of the brain has a set of characteristics that influence how the control center is trained. For instance, right sided memory is unique in that when it is activated we are not aware we are remembering. Each time we use a skill, we are remembering what we learned but that feels more like "knowing" because we don't need to remember where or how we learned the skill. The only way I can hold a glass of water and drink it is by learning how and then remembering. But when I hold my glass and drink I have no awareness of remembering, I just think, "I'm drinking." In the same way the control center remembers who we learned to be and how we learned to act but we do not think, "I am remembering who I am," we just think, "This is how I am" if we bother to think at all.

You might say the purpose of the brain's control center is *remembering how to act like myself under any conditions*. Said another way, its purpose is to keep me synchronized inside and out no matter what happens. What "happens" are emotions like joy, sadness, terror, rage, shame, disgust, despair and humiliation. Distressing states of emotion develop when there is a threat to our relationships and identities. Recovery skills will let a baby act in relational ways while they are very upset.

Sometimes these emotions arise from inside and sometimes they come from others around us. If our control center is ignorant or disorganized we lose control under these strong emotions. If our control center is strong and well trained we stay exactly the same no matter how intense these feelings get. The preparation for handling all that distress takes place before a baby's second birthday—if he has a good mom.

Let's take a quick tour of the four levels of the control center. Careful synchronization of brain activity is learned, in stages, by the four levels of the brain's control center. From bottom to top this remarkable structure is a learning machine. Level one forms our basic bonds. Our bonds are extremely specific and sensory. When level one wants mommy, daddy won't do. When it wants daddy, mommy gets pushed away. Level one is below the cortex so it has a will of its own. Level one determines when you are "in love" and who will not ring your chimes. Our deepest pains and joys come from level one. It is our bonding center. When it is *on* we want to attach. When it is *off* we don't. We could call level one our *attachment light* because when it is *on* our faces signal—I want you!

Like level one, level two is also below the cortex. Level two is our basic evaluation center. It has three different opinions about our experiences: good, bad and scary. Once level two has an opinion it can't be persuaded to change. It is the emotional brain for one and it only cares what it thinks. Unless you are in a rather deep coma, level two of your control center is always on.

Level three is the main synchronization area of the control center. It is cortex and open to interaction with other people—particularly those with whom we have bonded. Level three is the emotional brain for two people. It can synchronize with only one other person at a time. Level three does its basic growth and training by synchronizing with mother between two and nine months of age.

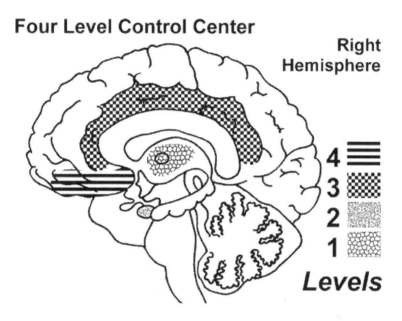

Figure 1 The Brain's Control Center

> **Figure 1** shows the brain structures most often associated with these four levels of the control center. There is still considerable uncertainty about where some functions start and stop but they seem to be centered in the areas shown on the chart. Level one uses the thalamus and what are known as *deep limbic structures* like the basal ganglia. Level two is centered in the amygdala. The cingulate cortex holds the "mother core" at level three. Best studied is the orbital prefrontal cortex at level four. Together these structures have been called the limbic system.

Level three synchronizes many things. By following a good mom's lead, level three learns to synchronize the lower and higher levels of the brain—those below the cortex with the cortex. Level three synchronizes the different lobes of the brain. It also synchronizes baby and mommy—one brain with another. This is why we call level three the "mother core" because it synchronizes the baby's level three with mother's level three. When mommy and baby are synchronized this way, mommy's third level is downloaded into the baby's "mother core." Mother's more developed brain duplicates itself in her baby including what mother knows and how her brain is built.

Level four is our conscious identity center. This is the part of the mind that thinks of itself as ME. We talked about level four in chapter two and gave it the name *right prefrontal cortex*. This area is also called the *right orbital prefrontal cortex* and even the *orbitofrontal cortex*. Here flexible thinking, moral behavior, personal preference and self-awareness reside. The prefrontal cortex knows it is ME who am active and living my life. It is the top level of the control center and, if the four levels are well trained and developed, level four will have the last word about what the brain and body will do. This level four "ability to maintain flexibly organized behavior in the face of high levels of arousal or tension"[1] is what development researcher Alan Sroufe calls "a central aspect of a stable individual." Level four is where the capacity for flexible organization operates.

SYNCHRONIZING "ATTACHMENT LIGHTS"

Synchronization does not just start at level three but much deeper in the brain. The many synchronization activities deep in the brain include forty cycle-per-second back-to-front signals originating from the thalamus, right-to- left cycles from the cerebellar vermis, heart rates, day and night cycles among the brain waves. The fast-track in the right brain runs around twelve cycles per second (back to front) in alert adults while conscious thoughts in the left brain run at five cycles (front to back.) Training a baby brain requires synchronizing with a bigger and better trained brain to learn these cycles. Level one of his control center picks who he will attach to for this training.

Baby starts by forming a strong bond with his or her brain trainer through a process called attachment. Deep inside the baby feels the impulse to attach as his bonding circuits switch on. This deep brain attachment activity shows on his face. We say, "His face lit up." Our

---

[1] L. Alan Sroufe, Emotional Development: the organization of emotional life in early years, (Cambridge: Cambridge University Press 1997) p. 159 [quoted in Daniel Siegel, The Developing Mind, (New York: Guilford Press 1999), p. 156]

term for this brain/body/face activity will be that the baby's attachment light is on. Everything hinges on what happens next.

Synchronized: When a baby wants to attach, he looks for eyes, he moves, he makes sounds that to a good mother-mind mean "my baby wants me." His attachment light is *on* so hers comes *on* too. When her baby has had enough for the moment he looks way, gets quiet and lets her know he needs quiet now. Mom follows his lead. His attachment circuits and hers go *on* and *off* together. His basic evaluation at level two of his control center feels, "this is good." With that, life is good and he is secure.

Always off: The baby whose attachment light comes *on* but no one responds is in for an excruciatingly painful time. Nothing in his life will ever hurt as much as having his attachment light ignored. We feel that kind of pain too when our dog is run over, our child dies or our mate runs away with our best friend. Since the child's need to connect is dismissed or unnoticed his basic evaluation level feels "bad." He will try to turn off his attachment light but since it is subcortical (with a mind of its own), it won't turn off.

Baby's second line of defense is to hide his attachment light. By his second year of life he can begin to fake what is socially acceptable and hide his real feelings. Now he will play quietly by himself and ignore his parents when they come and go. He appears independent and unemotional but inside his little heart is beating hard as he plays it cool.

By age thirteen all the outside traces of his pain will be masked so well he won't even know. His attachment level does not come on very often anymore. Only when it comes time to bond with a mate or children will the damage show. They too will get ignored and disregarded. He (or she) keeps his attachment light *off* so all his level-one functions are very undeveloped, ignorant, weak and unsynchronized.

Always on: This insecure style of attachment is known for its clingy, dependent and needy style. The funny thing is that unless you pay attention to synchronization, mothering that produces this kind of child are hard to distinguish from good mothering. The simple difference is this: good mothering synchronizes to the baby, bad mothering wants baby to synchronize with the adult. In the case of this bad mothering, parents are guided by their own attachment lights and memories of past attachment pains. An insecure and distracted mother looks for her baby when the mother's attachment light comes on and then wants the baby to turn his on also.

Whether his light is *off* or *on* is not that important to her, mommy comes when she needs closeness. She overlooks baby's attachment light signals because she is distracted by her own attachment needs. Slowly the baby learns to keep his attachment light *on* all the time because he never knows when she might come or leave again. Baby does not want to miss out on his only opportunity for a while. Unlike the "always off" baby who never seems to be upset, "always on" is always ready to whimper and slow to be soothed.

Chaotic: When the turning *on* of his attachment light produces unpredictable and scary reactions, the level two evaluation registers both good and bad at the same time. The baby boy begins to expect the approach of his mother as a scary event. He needs her. He wants her, but what happens to him when he gets her attention frightens him sometimes. He does not know how to solve this problem.

Three things can make a baby boy frightened of his own attachment light. His attachment signals produce frightening results if they: 1) make mom angry sometimes, 2) lead to his becoming overwhelmed by Mom's emotional needs (she needs him to make her happy) or 3) expose him to a mommy who is feeling scared and upset about something in life. Baby cannot deal with anything so bad that it is scaring mommy. Under these three conditions, when baby's attachment light comes *on* he fears pain but desires closeness simultaneously. Since he cannot know and cannot guess he becomes disorganized. What will happen this time? If we need help (say the police) but they are likely to shoot us, do we call? This baby begins to feel the same confusion about closeness. This unsolvable problem develops a life-long susceptibility to mental illness and poor relationships.

SYNCHRONIZING ENERGY LEVELS

When I was a boy ukuleles were really popular. I spent hours learning to play. For even the simplest song I would have to stop singing and put my fingers on the strings one at a time for the next chord. Sometimes I had to look up chords in a book before I could play them. A good musician could have played along with me easily if she had synchronized to my lack of skill by stopping when I needed to stop. I could never have played along with a good musician—at first that is.

After I got better, following the beat and speed of a good player would be just what I needed, but only after I learned the chords. I needed to have certain musical patterns very well learned and practiced before I could play a song smoothly let alone join a band and stay synchronized. A good music teacher would know that and so would a good mother.

As we have seen, the main characteristic of good mothering is that parents slow down, quiet themselves and match their baby's energy and ability. Level three of the control center is particularly suited for synchronizing these energy states. This area, known as the cingulate cortex or "mother core," is generally larger in women's brains. When a mother synchronizes her mother core with the same area in her baby's brain, the two quickly develop matching brain chemistry, matching brain patterns and finally matching brain structures. In other words, mama can download a working model of her own mother core system into her baby. This download is expected by the baby's brain between two and nine months of age through face-to-face interactions. Mother must pace herself because her baby can't match her speed with his immature and (at first) disorganized brain. If she trains him well, by nine months of age he can begin to keep synchronized himself.

Right-brain-to-right-brain: Synchronization is accomplished by right-brain-to-right-brain communication that is natural and easy if we have a working mother core. The short version of how this works is as follows: whatever our right brain feels is immediately and honestly displayed on the left side of our face. Anyone looking at our face will see the image of our left face and its emotions projected onto the left side of the retinas in both their eyes. The nerves from their left retinas lead immediately to the right side of their brains where their synchronization circuits are given the job of decoding the emotion on our face and responding. Their true response goes on the left side of their face and back to the right side of our brain in the same way. Six complete cycles of these messages pass through both brains each second. Each cycle is slightly amplified so the feelings grow stronger each time around.

Starting and stopping: The most obvious part of synchronizing is starting when our baby's attachment light comes on and stopping when he needs a break. This provides tremendous security to the baby. He does not need to fear being abandoned or overwhelmed. He can focus on learning how to make his brain do what Mommy's brain does. If Mommy had a good mother core, her brain will read his signals and know just when to start and when to stop.

Climbing together: When Mommy first sees her baby is ready to connect with her and link their right brains, she will usually be at a higher energy level than her baby. Her immediate response to linking minds will be to lower her arousal level to match her baby's. Her heart rate drops, her face relaxes until their minds are at the same energy level. Their joy climbs together until the baby's heart rate peaks, his mind can take no more joy. He looks away, disconnecting stimulation to his right brain. This process, which only took a few seconds because the communication is so good, so fast and so mutual, saw mom and baby match smiles, heart rates, brain chemistry while energy levels climb as high up as baby could make it. That is half the synchronization cycle. The second half is the descent.

This time Mom goes first and baby has to find his own way. Mom knows how to lower her energy levels quickly so she goes to a restful state almost immediately. Baby has to coast to a stop at first. He does not know how to quiet himself. Practice pays off again, however, because the more they practice being quiet together, the faster baby quiets. Being able to quiet himself when he is in an intense emotion will be a very useful skill. We all love to be with people who can become calm quickly when things go wrong. This ability to quiet oneself quickly is the strongest predictor of lifelong mental health. A control center that can't quiet itself is the best predictor of mental illness.

Working and resting: A mind that can start when it is supposed to start, stop when it is supposed to stop, get energized when energy is needed, quiet itself when things get too intense, and keep synchronized inside and out will have endurance, resilience and intelligence. By alternating working together and resting together *at the baby's pace* good mothering teaches a baby the rhythm of life and relationships. Now baby has the beat! Work together—rest together, smile together—rest together, cry together—recover together, first at his pace but as soon as he can keep up he will join the band. A control center with a well-trained third level can begin to initiate synchronizing with others by nine months of age. An untrained or incorrectly trained brain may always need others to synchronize with them and this kind of damage is passed from one generation to another. We have met people who are usually hyperactive or depressed. They do not synchronize their energy states with others effectively.

Bad mothering: What a heavy-sounding term! All of us provide bad mothering at moments or with certain feelings. To a great extent, how well we do as mothers depends on what we received—particularly in our first three years of life. When a mother's control center is weak, disorganized or untrained, she will find her baby's natural disorganization very bothersome. Instead of getting involved with his mind, the deficient mother must struggle to maintain her own stability. Sometimes she does this by staying distant, uninvolved and ignoring his cues. She says, "He'll be fine," or "It's no big deal."

A second way a damaged mother keeps herself regulated is to make her baby follow her lead. She tries to "tidy him up" emotionally so he feels what she thinks he should feel. If that worked she would feel more in control. This is the mother who does everything "right" and makes her baby synchronize to her. These controlling mothers usually smile more, play more and get more involved with their children than do healthy mothers. Unregulated mothers want to be in class with their children. They stay involved, close, affectionate, warm, happy and God knows what other wonderful things so their baby will be happy. Their children do not learn how to synchronize themselves, quiet themselves, or get back to joy from distress quickly.

The third kind of bad mothering is the "just make it stop" type. She is out of control in a very obvious way due to a blown control center, drugs or overwhelming circumstances. Because she wants "it" to stop she sometimes forces or scares her baby into stopping his emotional demands on her. She explodes at his upsets. "Just shut up!"

What these three types of defective mother cores have in common is that they cannot focus on their child, read their baby's cues or synchronize to their baby. They can't match baby's energy levels and his rhythm because their own signals are too faint, too strong or too disorganized.

THE TOP COMMAND CENTER LEVELS

Timing is deeply important to good brain function. Learning what to synchronize and what to leave out is fundamental for using our heads. A strong and well-trained control center stays synchronized when handling intense feelings. While the control center is working well, the right orbital prefrontal cortex now has "executive control" capacity over the rest of the brain. An immature, poorly trained, weakened or chemically disrupted control center falls apart internally. The layers become "delaminated" one layer at a time starting with the top.

When distressing emotions begin to flood the brain the first desynchronization occurs when the right-sided-control-center no longer provides clear identity messages for the left hemisphere. Upset feelings take all the right brain's attention. The focused thoughts and words of the left brain wander or focus on details and miss the big picture. Some people disconnect. Some people become reactive.

A reliable indication that the right prefrontal cortex (rPFC) is in trouble will be a loss of our best self. Level four contains the capacities of the self – our identity – allowing us to act like ourselves rather than become disorganized. The first losses will be level four functions. When level four is shut off, all the following abilities are temporarily lost.

- Personal identity
- Emotional regulation (individual and mutual)
- Joint-focused attention
- Switching focus of attention
- Three-way bonds
- Personal preferences
- Creativity
- Satisfaction
- Goal directed behavior
- Moral and social behavior
- Correcting our interpretations of others
- Time travel / age regression (remembering who we are over time)
- Calming/controlling the amygdala (level two)

The right orbital prefrontal cortex relies upon the level three "mother core" to provide it with a good picture of the current emotional situation. The rPFC (top level of the brain's control center), runs well as long as the level just below it (level three) can stay synchronized. The level three (cingulate) must have enough electrical and chemical capacity to handle this storm in the brain. If the emotional storm becomes too strong the control center continues desynchronizing.

Level three, or the synchronization layer, shuts off the top (identity) layer when distress reaches intensities where there is no developed capacity to climb or quiet. More nerves are firing or firing faster than this brain is trained to manage. Now that the brain has reached a state where it has no previous mastery, it begins looking for ONE mind greater than itself. He or she needs one mind with which to synchronize that has handled this kind of nerve storm. He needs one mind that can show him the way to handle an upset feelings this big. Mental flexibility is gone, he must find the ONE.

Babies frequently become overwhelmed with feelings and desperately need someone who will help them get back under control. The mother core looks for someone with capacity and experience to synchronize with him right-brain-to-right-brain and provide an example of being this upset, staying in a relationship and still acting like the same person he or she always was. Synchronization with this "mother" will allow him to synchronize with his higher (prefrontal) brain functions again. A mother with a well-developed capacity could give him training now that will improve his control center. While this chapter deals with babies, the same need can arise at any point in life.

If synchronization of the mother core with a greater ONE fails, the basic evaluation layer (level two) goes to terror and just tries to make it all stop. This subcortical emergency level is always on. Positive desires are forgotten and the baby switches to fear, withdrawal and avoidance. Gone is moral behavior. Gone is creativity and mental flexibility. This child is now in a high stress state where everything is focused on making it stop. If emotions get intense enough, level two will switch off all possible areas of the brain and declare an energy-conservation-withdrawal-shut-down of all systems. Our baby is now in shock. His control center is desynchronized entirely and he is in trouble.

The alternative to meltdowns is helping babies grow strong control centers. During infancy a baby takes a slowly pulsing mass of cells and transforms them into a synchronized working brain. Baby learns to synchronize the different parts. The infant learns to synchronize himself with others. They learn to synchronize words and feelings, effort and rest, relationships and emotions, and asking and receiving. If all goes well, by age four a baby is ready to start taking care of himself. No longer must life be synchronized to him in the ways his nursery provided for him. Now he is ready to begin matching the rhythms of a community. But, suppose this baby's body reaches the age of four while his personality development is still too immature, disorganized, ignorant or incomplete?

DEFECTIVE AND WEAK BONDS

Pity the poor baby whose mother does not sense his needs or respond well to them. She feeds him when she is hungry, or sends him to play when she wants to watch television and holds him when she needs reassurance. He will not learn his needs or his feelings. Instead, he learns his mother's needs and feelings in a way that makes him feel compelled to meet them. Her mommy-sized needs and feelings will overwhelm a baby because his baby-sized identity disintegrates under such pressure. To survive, he begins a search for someone who will pay attention to *him or her*.

The baby with weak or fearful bonds senses his desperate need to be connected and lets it be known in various ways. He doesn't understand that his search for attention is a request. Remember that babies must even be taught that their cry is a request. The child who seeks attention has not learned to ask for what he needs. This is usually obvious to adults who say correctly, "He is just looking for attention." Attention is exactly what he craves. If he has not been taught to meet his needs by asking, then he invents other ways to attract attention from his mother or anyone. Maybe he will find what he needs, maybe he will get beat up, or maybe he will get molested. Most likely, he will just get disliked. He is not ready for weaning. He cannot take care of himself.

The poorly bonded baby is in trouble before he reaches the end of infancy. As the time to start taking care of himself approaches, he continues to feel a desperate need to be connected because he hasn't forged a strong bond with his mother. He senses that closeness to others will meet his needs, but his bond with mother is not strong enough to bring satisfaction or security. For them, weaning will feel like further abandonment and rejection.

Because it is so upsetting to be abandoned and rejected, an infant with defective bonds will reject his or her new identity at weaning. Instead of welcoming the goal of taking care of himself, he will try to trick people into taking care of him. He will stay at infant maturity because weak or defective bonds have crippled his identity. This malnutrition-of-the-soul is quite traumatic. Because of it, the baby lacks the necessary good things he requires to grow properly. The development of a boy's brain is more seriously damaged (according to brain scan studies) by neglect than by abuse. We call this absence of good things—type A trauma. The absence of good things will block growth just as child abuse, illness and catastrophe will do. We call these bad things, type B trauma. In theory, both type A and B traumas can be overcome but it is much better to prevent them.

As baby is now approaching the transition to being a child our next chapter will look at the final preparations for what has traditionally been called weaning. A weaned child no longer depends entirely on its mother to sustain life. A weaned child still needs a mother.

Chapter Six
Babies and Parents

So Sarah laughed to herself as she thought, "After I am worn out and my lord is old, will I now have this pleasure?" Genesis 18:12NIV

With a full stack of blueberry pancakes in front of me, I felt particularly useless. A humorless nurse had just sent me away while my wife got "prepped" for an induced labor. Nurses had no use for a dad.

Very few fathers were allowed into the labor room in the early seventies. Even fewer fathers entered the delivery room. When they were admitted, Dads were kept in a corner. Doctors had no use for fathers when it came to babies and births.

Our doctor took the radical step of allowing me to stay by my wife for the whole birth, but only after a very careful screening. When our due date passed, the doctor scheduled us for a Monday morning birth-by-appointment. Well, it might not be quite right to say he scheduled *us* exactly, I was, more-or-less, the transportation.

Our doctor himself was still in bed when we arrived at the hospital that Monday morning so the nurses locked me out of the labor room. I protested that I had a special doctor's clearance to be present. That got me a steel-cold glare, a closed door and instructions to go get breakfast—or just do something.

I found the nearby Beaver Grill and got the North-country special. Across the counter, the cafeteria cook stayed busy with his work. He was oblivious to my becoming a father. He had sausage to fry. People ate, pulled on their Paul Bunyan jackets, Co-op caps and left. For them it was just an ordinary day. As for me, I have ordered blueberry pancakes every March seventeenth since then.

When the last fat blueberry was gone, I headed back toward the labor room. I felt my apprehension rising as I got closer. My first child would be here any minute, and I didn't want to miss it. I wanted to know everything about them. Anticipation was intense. I wanted to meet the life I had helped form. What if I passed out like they said fathers do? My vague uneasiness about being in a hospital got stronger when I saw Kitty connected to tubes.

"Stay out of the way," the nurse ordered as she left.

Once labor started, we stayed busy breathing. Rubbing sore muscles made me feel useful. Being the official timekeeper for contractions and intervals also gave me a reason to exist. My wife was clearly appreciative of my presence, which is more than some men can say. I sensed in her instructions to keep rubbing that there was room and need for me to be a husband, but what would I do as a father?

The doctor checked me over one last time before we went into the delivery room. "You can always leave if this gets to be too much," he said.

Kitty didn't have that option. I wanted to say something like, "If she can take it the least I can do is watch," but I kept my mouth shut and nodded.

Our son Jamie arrived by late afternoon. I was elated to be a witness to something so marvelous. The doctor ushered in this new life then held him up by his neck and the feet. We tried to catch glimpses of him between the green outfits of the medical team on the far side of the room. They wheeled him out one door and my wife out another. I followed her like a puppy on a leash—staying out of the way. Kitty asked about our baby and was told we would see Jamie at feeding time.

WHAT IS A DAD FOR?

My first job as a father was asking the nursing staff if it was feeding time yet. I was like the kid in the back seat asking, "Are we there yet?" By the third time I asked, we were there or perhaps the nurses had grown tired of me. Then, for a moment after he was fed, I held my son. Almost immediately the curtain was pulled back, a nurse pounced and carried him away. I kissed Kitty, took off my funny robe, and went home.

As I called all the relatives to tell them the news, the same question was asked by everyone, "How are the mother and baby?" There was lots to tell, but by eleven o'clock that night not one person had noticed I was now a dad. I began to wonder whether it mattered. What did it mean to be the father anyway?

It got worse from there. I awoke one night from a dead sleep to find myself being rolled over the edge of the bed and onto the floor. My wife had awakened and, after failing to find the baby, concluded that I must be lying on him. That got me a quick trip to the floor. Only then did Kitty remember that she had put Jamie back in his crib. She ran to find him while I tried to retrieve my breath and wits enough to say, "What on earth!?"

Breast-feeding also did nothing to help me find out what a father was for, except that Kitty took all my handkerchiefs and used them to catch drips! I can see why some men go out and buy the baby a baseball glove or a football, it gives a guy something to hold on to.

My favorite moments were when the little guy was sleeping. After I was sure he was still breathing, I'd stay and watch him until those little eyes finally opened and he would just gaze at me. There was nothing else in the world right then—just the two of us.

It seems Mommy was wired to know when he woke up, because before long she would call out, "Check and see if Jamie is awake yet."

"He is."

"Oh! Bring him here." And the mystery moment was over. I could feel something receding from my face into a lost inner pool the way water drains from the bathtub.

At first, I thought that picking up a baby was like handling high explosives. A quick motion might set something off, or maybe I might drop him and bring disaster. Streams of advice from the ladies did not build my confidence. They gathered like mosquitoes when I got near him. Kitty gave the play-by-play and Aunt Karen added the color commentary.

"Look at the way he holds the head. Not like that! Here, let me show you," my wife said.

"Men!" said her sister, "Don't they know a baby won't break?"

"Well, if they don't break, then what was wrong with how I held his head?" I wondered.

I felt cheated. There didn't seem to be much a father could do, or at least do right. Do babies even need fathers? Maybe fathers are for the time when children grow up, speak, walk, and go fishing.

If I didn't find some purpose as a father it was clear that I'd soon be out of the flow of life in this house—relegated to running errands and paying bills. Something inside me burned with desire to know why I was here. It was time I discovered what dads were for before life became a series of quick trips to the floor and lonely stacks of blueberry pancakes. Necessity may be the mother of invention, but desire is the father of discovery.

Dads are for discovery. Whereas mothers seem to focus on taking care of babies, Dads want the baby to do something. A baby represents so much potential. A dad wants to see his baby in action. I certainly wanted to discover what my baby could do. After all, it wasn't that many years since I took my dad's Chevy Impala out to see what it could do. A scary thought to some, I suppose.[1]

Now when it comes to *action* babies can seem a little unimpressive at first. Fathers and babies discover mouths, noses, hair, movement and noises. Once his child can hold up her head, Dad throws the baby up in the air to discover flying. Together they bounce, run, race and see what fun feels like. They discover what can be lifted, pushed, and jumped on, even when they must strain to do it. Together they find expression for the life that the child has received. Why, even the baby wants to discover things! Together the father and child will discover the world. They will learn how to protect, serve and enjoy the earth. Dad is a bridge to the wider world. They will learn to live off the land.

Without Dad's help, Mother might well become the baby's whole world. Dad soon becomes proof that Mom can't understand everyone all the time and Mom becomes proof that Dad, for all his power, can't move everything. Through Dad the baby can see that there is no need to be afraid of being connected to Mother. Dad's eagerness to be with his baby and playful competition for Mother's attention gives proof of this.

Furthermore, the boy need not fear that his mother (and after her all women) will control him or overpower his weak efforts at becoming an individual. His connection with Dad lets him be different than Mom and yet appreciated and admired. The boy can treasure closeness without fear and seek independence with enthusiasm. Girls can see that it is very good to be a girl. How dads treasure and protect their wives and babies has huge future implications. Hopeful girls grow where women and babies are treasured.

UNIQUENESS OF THE FATHER BOND

Dad forms a special connection with his child. When you think about it, this alone is a remarkable event. Unlike Mother, who risked her life just to give birth, who carried the child inside her for nine months, who fed her baby from her body, slept with the infant, and sensed his or her needs and feelings, Dad must bond because someone said to him, "Behold your child." Mother's bond was conditioned by a release of

---

[1] It could do about 135 mph. (The guys reading this wanted to know. The ladies are back to the paragraph about babies by now thinking, "Why can't men...something or another.")

oxytocin[1] when her baby was born. Mama gets more doses of this bonding chemical each time her baby nurses, but dad must bond almost entirely by visual and external means. Fortunately men bond more easily than women. This is good news and bad news. If men do not learn to guard their visual bonding tendencies, they will not form stable multigenerational communities.

The baby's first connections to mother surround him or her and engulf them. Babies connect to Mom by taking her breast in their mouth. Dad is an outside force that moves them up and down and throws them in the air. Dad connects and disconnects. Dad puts demands on their bodies. Dad is the destination Mom chooses for their first steps. With Dad they must be their own person. Dad in turn richly appreciates each thing that makes the baby an individual person.

Appreciation, anticipation, holding, comfort, and play are some of the first gifts a father gives to a child. These activities produce a bond between the father and his daughter or son that will grow and enrich both of their lives. Early appreciation of his child helps prepare the father in a unique way. He will be a far better guide for his child because he learned to appreciate the baby's characteristics from the very start.

Bonding with his baby is not free from turbulence. The average American first-time father must overcome a bit of resentment. In cultures where men do not depend so exclusively on their wives to meet all their emotional needs there is less of a crisis for men when Mama has a baby. To a man with infant maturity, this baby has taken away his wife's attention and affection. The baby now has her breasts. Mommy is too tired for hubby. Sex is something you check for with ultrasound scans.

Not too surprisingly, many men have their first affair while their wives are having their first baby. They get attached to a babe instead of a baby. No one gave them a "heads-up" about their attachment needs so as the result of having an ignorant and badly trained brain, these men never knew they were about to crave connection and it could get them in trouble.

Because a father with an untrained mind feels these nameless, vague but extremely intense and powerful urges to give life, a power beyond his own plans pushes him to bond. He must participate in receiving and giving life. He must join the dance of joy. Someone must light up to see him, be glad to be with him and want all he has to give. A man who has

---

[1] This powerful little peptide is the same chemical that lets women have multiple orgasms.

been trained to be a father knows he is getting ready to bond with his son or daughter. The untrained brain is an easy fish to catch and filet.

BABY AND FATHER

The "mother core" brain training a dad received from his mother many years ago (when he was a baby) is crucial for a dad to bond with his baby. A well-trained control center will let dad synchronize with his baby, bond with his baby, build joy with his baby and let dad calm himself enough to match what his baby needs. A good dad must be able to do both excitement and calm. The dad who can calm himself and calm others is way ahead of the game. He can use his brain.

Unfortunately for me, when my babies were born I had an ignorant brain. My wife's brain also had little idea what fathers were for so much of the bonding between me and my babies was left to chance. This meant that when mommy was not available and daddy had to take care of the babies the boys were hard to comfort. They were not securely attached to me, my face, my smell or my voice. It was hard for me to calm my babies when they got upset.

For this section we will call the baby "her" since English lacks a term for both genders. This way we can use "him" for father and "her" for babies of either gender.

The baby who discovers dad early in life discovers a wonderful thing. This creature is the one her mother, the visible source of her life, waits and seeks. He is harder, hairier, usually bigger than Mom. He appears and disappears in an almost random way. Dad represents the unpredictable, the exciting, the one who brings change. Being up on Daddy's shoulders is like riding an elephant or driving a fast car. It is awesome how much power the girl can control and direct. It is here the baby begins to learn of meekness.

The story is told of a Greek general with Alexander the Great who wrote home about his new warhorse. It was, he said, the strongest horse he had ever had. The beast would run tirelessly and yet was guided by the lightest touch, a truly meek horse.

Wrestling with Dad, or riding on his back, wrapping little arms around his head and nearly poking out his eyes, the baby begins to learn of meekness. To her, Dad is great power under sensitive control. This teaches her to use her will wisely by imitating her father's self-control. Baby can stay safe and still have fun.

Babies look to father for examples of how to handle their feelings. Dads have a place in teaching a baby how to climb Joy Mountain and calm back down. Dads also help babies climb the more rugged emotional mountains and calm down safely. Emotions are the most powerful forces a baby knows and dad sets a clear example of how to survive and use these powerful forces. When the baby is afraid, in a rage, or even in pain, her father's assuring closeness lets the baby know that it will be okay. Together, a family must explore the whole mountain range of different feelings. The family must also rest in calm valleys if they want to develop good survival skills. Of course, parents must have earned their maturity.

To a baby, her father's eyes reveal the meaning of what the world does to her. This right-brain-to-right-brain-communication-link helps make sense of emotional experiences. Seeing dad's reaction to a fall lets her know if it was serious. Seeing dad's reaction to mommy leaving lets her know that dad "has his lights on" and knows what is happening. Dad's look will tell her if Dad knows what is happening to her, too. If there is a bond to Dad, baby will use Dad's brain to help her calm down when things go wrong.

Baby and his or her body. Boys learn to use their bodies, walk their bodies, sit their bodies, dress their bodies, feed their bodies like Daddy does. Daddy has the body most like his. Boys learn the limits of their bodies and how to take care of their needs from watching how Daddy does it. Dad, the chap with a body most like his own, is there to help the boy learn to live in his body. And whether or not the aunts think highly of how these two start out, it is Dad who is best equipped to show the boy what he can do.

I remember one little boy picking up the communion wafer at church and saying in a loud voice, "What the hell kind of bread is this?" His dad wanted to hide. The opposite can also happen. Another dad "busted his buttons" when Junior pushed his plastic lawn mower around the yard.

Girls also come to understand their bodies from Dad's responses. Her body does athletic and fun things. Girls must be more careful with sports that impact her head as the brain structures in girl's heads are not quite as jolt-resistant as boys who can also easily be injured. But, everyone is learning to take safe risks and stretch limits.

Problems develop from placing too much importance on either performance or attractiveness. Dad's appreciation of how she has fun on good days and bad days – just because she did it – gives her freedom.

His responses to her comparisons with others or with her own expectations help her experience that what makes her special is always there.

It might be hard to think about bodies this way but much of the issue with bodies comes down to who "owns" them. It is much more widely accepted that boys "own" their own bodies. Boy's bodies are there for them to use. Girls, however, are frequently left feeling that everyone who looks at them owns her body. Her body is there to please others and not for her to live in as her own. Dad is there to insist that it is her body. She can "try out" her own body and see what it can do and how she wants to use it for her own satisfaction.

Self-expression. The bond with father teaches self-expression, how to play, work, make things change, and influence their environment. Babies and children need two influences. On one hand they are the people Mom taught them to be with needs and feelings and receive from others. On the other hand they can also make a change in the world around them. With Dad's help they can do things and make things happen. Even before weaning, this fatherly influence begins to produce a rich variety of expression.

Dad is very interested in what abilities the baby has inside and wants to try them out. Together they see if she can run fast, catch a ball, ride a bike, drive the car while sitting on Dad's lap, jump, climb or shoot a basket. It is said that when Bach would sit down at a new organ he would take it to the limits and see what sort of "lungs" it had. Dads do that. Together he and his baby will explore and expand the limits of her world. With Dad the baby will come into full possession of her body and mind. Together they will play. They don't have to test the limits, they just want to.

Making mistakes. Around Dad things are always going wrong. The baby learns that Dad smiles when he tries and misses. Together they laugh at mistakes. Together they test the limits to see what is possible today. Together the baby learns to stretch her limits but also how to set limits as well. She can clearly see the difference in power between herself and her dad. She can't do everything Dad can yet.

Because her father cares, a baby can see that her efforts mean something, even when they fail. It will come as no surprise to the reader that men are failure prone in most of their efforts. For a baby to grow up into an adult, they must also get good at failure. One of the essential ingredients of a good childhood is the opportunity to fail without being penalized.

Freedom to fail is a big part of preventing addictions, particularly sexual ones. When a babies grow up with freedom to fail they will allow real relationships to nurture their souls instead of living in fantasy game or self-generated sexuality. We will get back to this in the next book *Growing Us: becoming an adult.*

MOTHERS AND FATHERS TOGETHER

Each member of a family exerts his or her influence. Individual uniqueness prevents us from making accurate generalizations about each family member's role, but some generalizations about mothers and fathers will help us divide the work of parenting according to who might be better at a given task. This difference between a mother and a father is mostly a difference in emphasis and speed. Mothers and fathers tend to divide tasks according to who does it faster or better.

Babies don't leave much time. We still laugh at my wife's idea when our first child was born that when she stayed home, she would have time for projects she had always wanted to do. Time is the critical factor when there are babies at home. This means that whoever is faster will usually get the job.

Differences between mothers and fathers. INTUITION or knowing what others need and feel, is required to guess what babies need. This intuition develops from a flow of mutual mind states in the fast track of the right brain. These mutual mind states run faster than conscious thought. Men usually lose their intuition and sensitivity if they are doing anything that requires the slower conscious concentration. The most intuitive of men may become oblivious of others when he is trying to sort the mail, cook a meal or plan his day. Women, on the other hand, can often do these tasks and still maintain their sensitivity. Consequently, a mother can usually wash the dishes and watch the kids, while a dad can only manage one or the other.

A father may not always be less intuitive than a mother. It is not that fathers totally lack a capacity to sense what a child is feeling or what they need. Fathers can provide these functions quite well, but they must focus and take the time. The average man will just be slower than the average woman. He may also need to stop whatever else he is doing at the time.

This also gives some hope to single parents who must do everything themselves. The good news is you can do it. The bad news is some things will take you longer and single parents are already trying to do the work of two. This is another place where it is particularly important to recruit other people as supplemental parents.

EXERTION or finding the limits of what we can do, is required for babies' growth. Fathers' abilities to focus on tasks help them take children out of their comfort zone. This capacity to focus also helps them guide children back to joy after a failure or minor injury. Fathers help children build faith in their ability to recover after something goes wrong. Mothers, who can see that something like this would happen, are often more reluctant to try. Mothers are usually more comforting while fathers are planning the next failure.

These are generalizations and in some families parents are quite the opposite of what I have just described. Although men and women can each do almost all the same things the other can, no man will be a natural mother and no woman a natural father. Children are simply so complex that they will receive everything both parents can invest. Children can live on almost any kind of food: fried, sugary, processed, even partly decayed but we actually want them to have the best not just what will let them survive. Therefore, we want to let the caregivers with the best models in a particular area engage with their children.

Both parents are needed sometimes. Between two parents babies learn to come and go without separation anxiety. They are always aware of going *to* a joyful face more than they are aware of going *away* from the other parent. Two parents reduce the baby's fears in many other ways as well. Baby learns to receive from his mother and to create from her father. Mother clears the way for the baby to know what he needs and feels because Mum is not afraid of his feelings or demands. Father helps the baby to grow past her fear of failure by enjoying failing together. The baby learns what she can do as well as where her limitations lie.

From the parent's attention and stories a baby learns that she or he has great value. What she takes in does not give her value. What he makes happen does not give him value. He doesn't do these things to get value or love, they are just part of who he is. Her connections with Mom and Dad let her know the value of "just being me." This is the goal of infancy.

We tell stories. As soon as a baby can toddle about, stories become the most important way to keep the family synchronized. Stories are the vehicle that makes our minds understandable to others.[1] The stories I

[1] Dr. Siegel makes this point over and over. Daniel Siegel and Mary Hartzell, Parenting from the Inside Out, (New York, NY: Penguin Random House,2004), pp. 31-35, 40-41, 43-45, 268-273.

mean are the "stories-of-us" that created and maintain our identity as individuals and families. Parents tell these stories to each other. Together, parents help a baby to tell these stories. The stories-of-us help our minds learn to remember who we are and how we act.

- Stories-of-us help us make sense of the world. *"Daddy loves to play golf! When you get a little bigger you can play too."*
- Stories-of-us let us feel close to each other, learn to trust and understand, and even fix things that went wrong. *"I'm sorry I scared you with my yelling. A lizard ran down my neck!"*
- Stories help us share joy with those who were not there. *"You'll never believe where we went after school..."*
- Stories help us bring home "owies" to be comforted. *"I lost my favorite jacket."*
- Stories help us learn from others. *When I was your age... (Yeah! Like that is going to work!)*

Every day in every life needs to become a story. If you own a mind, you need stories to synchronize all the parts of your mind and make sense of life. *"When something goes wrong in our family we talk it out until we can all be glad to be together again. That is what families are for— helping each other. Mommy is mad because I promised to call and I forgot, so I need to talk to her now and make it better."*

Daddy's stories help baby understand mommy. *"Mommy is going to be right back. She just went to take your sister to school. She didn't forget you wanted to have breakfast so she made your favorite non-sweetened whole-grain granola, tofu and spinach salad puree."*

Mommy's stories help baby understand daddy. *"Daddy would like to give you rides, honey but he hurt his back roughhousing with Uncle Mike and now he has to stay in bed all day until his back gets better."*

Mommy and daddy's stories help grandma and grandpa understand baby. *"See that! His molars are starting to come in! He is just fussy, but last night he seemed to like sucking on a cold chew ring."* Grandma and grandpa's stories help everyone understand the family—and sometimes drive everyone nuts.

One of the best tests of whether someone had a good family is how well they tell the stories of their childhood. The better the family, the more complete and truthful the stories they tell. Of course, they also do better at making themselves understood and understanding others.[1] Mommy and Daddy must work together to help their baby see the other parent through their eyes—by means of stories. Reading stories to your children helps them to learn even more perspectives.

THE FATHER-AND-CHILD WEANING BOND

As weaning approaches, Dad becomes a larger player in his baby's life. Dad is a good place to practice what baby has learned from Mother. Mother has been teaching how to ask for what baby needs. When baby practices on Dad the results are remarkable. Dad responds to his baby's requests. What a wonderful world!

Dad is also the model for the little child. As they begin exploring the world together, his baby notices that Dad also asks people for what he needs and they give it to him. Asking and receiving are keys to living off the land the child is entering. The baby knows that this enormous person is a picture what he or she will be like when they get big. Just following the future around is fascinating.

Dad is very important in helping a child meet her needs. He will teach his child how to live off the land. This becomes the focus of a father's training once the day of weaning arrives.

In more traditional cultures, weaning is a specific time when breast-feeding stops, but for us it means the child is ready to feed and care for herself. In our culture, little trail markers signal its approach; like the day she holds her own spoon, ties her own shoes, puts on her own clothes and gets into bed on her own. These are all parts of weaning in the sense that I am using the word.

Benjamin had a special baby bottle burying ceremony. He and his dad dug a hole in the back yard. His older sister held the bottles until it was time to throw them in. Mommy brought his favorite cake and ice cream and the whole family partied. Other families have done the same with diapers.

Weaning is the second great transformation in a child's identity. The first metamorphosis occurred at birth and was almost entirely based on his mother's efforts. Weaning is the first major achievement that mother, father and child reach as a family team, and what an achievement it is.

As children enter their new identity their joyful identity brain center (right prefrontal cortex) undergoes a new growth spurt. Dad's joy in his

---

[1] Siegel and Hartzell, pp. 48-50.

child will result in a euphoric new bond. The child enters the "like father—like child" phase. As the African proverb says, "He who walks with his father will soon be like him."

Early weaning. Unfortunately, we tend to rush self-care. If we start too soon our baby will not make an identity change. Instead she will come to believe that independence gives her value. She will continue to think of herself as being what she does.

Even if weaning gets rushed a little, each step is part of our child's history and should be fully celebrated. If all went well during infancy, the baby has learned to "take in" energy from his mother and to "put out" energy from her father. When he or she turns four we can celebrate his new identity together as a family and community.

Traditional weaning. When Isaac was weaned Abraham held a feast. The day of his son's weaning was community news and everyone was invited. It was the boy's introduction to his community and their introduction to the boy. The feast made it clear that this child was important, under his father's care and protection and in need of the community's involvement. The feast let everyone know that while the boy had depended on his mother until then, his father was now in charge of his nutrition. Even as his mother brought him into the world through her labor, the father now brought him into the world surrounded by the fruit of his labor—the delightful flavors of living off the land.

Isaac began to learn how to ask for what he needed from others. At the feast there was plenty of food to help him learn. For the boy it meant that he was now able to feed himself and everyone was happy about this achievement. He was one of a people now and past his first major hurdle, thanks to his mother's excellent training.

A child who could feed themselves was ready for bigger adventures, and everyone rejoiced. This introduced him to the goal for the child stage—learning to care of oneself. For this a child needs a family and community. Children do not feed themselves in isolation. A feast meant that all the community celebrated and rejoiced that they too could feed themselves.

Fathers and weaning. Weaning is Dad's day in much the same way that the birth day is Mother's day. Special changes in a child's identity take place on weaning day that involve Dad in unique ways.

Comforted by his father's voice and surrounded by his father's ample supply, the children who can feed themselves are now ready to learn many new ways to meet their needs. Buying, growing, building, finding, stalking, thinking, gathering, chasing, and waiting are all ways that their father meets his needs and soon the children will learn to do the same.

At weaning the father's role begins in earnest as he takes children into the wider world. Each trip goes farther from the familiar base camp of her mother, but with Dad's help the children discover new supply sources. Together they are living off the land.

THE SECOND
METAMORPHOSIS

*

THE CHILD STAGE

*

LIVING IN GRACE

CHILD
The Child Stage
IDEAL AGE
Four to Twelve

NEEDS
•Weaning
•Help doing what they don't feel like doing
•Help sorting feelings, imaginations and reality
•Feedback on guesses, attempts and failures
•Love they do not have to earn
•Be taught their family history
•Be taught the history of God's family
•Be taught the "big picture" of life
•

TASKS
•Take care of themselves
•Learn to ask for what they need
•Learn self-expression
•Develop their personal resources and talents
•Learn to make themselves understandable to others
•Learn to do hard things
•Tame their cravings
•Learn what satisfies
•See themselves through the "eyes of heaven"
•

Chapter Seven
Becoming a Child

Our tent was pitched on a slightly level spot between a tree and a rock, one day's hike into the Golden Trout Wilderness. This was our first backpack trip ever. Most of the junior high group from church were scattered around us eating and complaining heartily. Jamie lay in the tent feeling sick.

We steamed macaroni and cheese in a coffee can. Most of the kids ate some. Jamie stayed in the tent. Rami poked at his food but ate almost nothing. When ten and eleven-year-old boys aren't eating, something is wrong. I felt sort of nauseated myself. Were we coming down with something out here in the middle of nowhere?

"Drink a little water and get some rest. You will probably feel better in the morning," I said stuck halfway into the tent like a Pooh Bear.

"I'm not thirsty."

Like childhood, learning to camp in the wilderness requires us to learn many new skills. Each backpacker needed to be able to take care of themselves. One must stay on trails, find shelter, carry all necessary supplies, not carry too much weight, avoid dangers and animals (like bears), prepare meals, stay healthy, and find safe water to drink. This last task was accomplished on our first trip with iodine tablets that gave the water an unpleasant flavor but killed the parasites and germs.

Getting boys to drink water with iodine proved to be harder than making them clean their rooms at home. Some vacation! The next day it was the same, and the next. By the third day Rami started eating and drinking a little. My appetite returned the fourth day. The main problem was that without food the boys were weak and lacked energy to climb mountains and explore. All the same, we did learn to backpack.

The High Sierra was beautiful, the trip was so much fun that we decided to go again. This time, I did more reading in preparation. To my surprise, the section on high-altitude health listed nausea, loss of appetite and lack of thirst as symptoms of *dehydration*, a common mountain health hazard. I assumed that if we weren't thirsty, we weren't dehydrated but that was not true. Sometimes we need exactly what we don't feel like having.

Other symptoms of dehydration included swelling of the fingers and extremities. We had each experienced those problems on the first day's climb. But who would think that dehydration could make us swell? I would have guessed it might make us shrivel! Sometimes a problem produces exactly the opposite effects from what we expect. There is a lot a child doesn't know about self-care.

The iodine in the water kept us from getting sick from parasites but because it made us avoid the water it also led us to getting sick. Sometimes a solution produces a new problem. Taking care of oneself is not that easy. On our first trip we did not know how to make sense of the symptoms of dehydration so we did not drink enough water to correct it. As a result we lost several days of enjoyment, but if the days had been a little hotter the problem could have become life threatening.

By not drinking enough water we lacked a necessary good thing. The lack of something necessary for survival and development is called a type A trauma. The Absence of something needed. Often we cannot recognize what is missing from our symptoms. Sometimes we don't even want what we need, just like we avoided water with a bad taste and got dehydrated. Missing some necessary ingredients for development is the most common problem during childhood. In this chapter we will examine the steps necessary to reach the goal of childhood—taking care of oneself. There is a lot a child does not know.

WEANING—A NEW IDENTITY

Childhood begins at weaning. The child leaves infancy behind and with it his identity as a baby. Babies believe that others would always take care of them. After weaning children learn how they can take care of themselves. This change radically reshapes the way children understand themselves. Their identities have changed. A child is transformed and knows it.

This first transformation from one identity to another proves that transformation is possible and good. Transformations are more like a leap than a step. Other transformations throughout life can be faced without fear. Each transformation will bring a new, unknown, and larger self. Leaving an old identity for a new one is an adventure. Instead of repairing old, outgrown identities, we eagerly become someone greater. Weaning is that kind of change.

Four-year-olds are especially well positioned for big changes. Trust in parents is almost total so they will follow instructions and jump. Strong, joyful babies will make the leap just to see their parents smile. They are almost fearless because they do not understand enough to be daunted. Without a successful weaning at four when they are confident, children will become afraid to leave their identities behind for new ones later on in life. In the future, those stuck in infancy will defend their baby ways instead of transforming into adults, parents and elders. We should note that many, if not most, men in America are not ready to take the leap.

CHILDHOOD GOALS

Exploration. "Why?" begins with childhood. "Why are you big?" "Why do ducks have feathers?" Children begin exploring their world, trying to understand what they see. Babies can explore their relationships, bodies and homes, but children are ready to explore the world.

Imagination. From four to six children live in a world of imagination. Even the way young children understand themselves is built on what they imagine.[1] Young children can imagine far easier then they can understand the complex reality around them. Their explanations are fantastic and fun. Four to six year old children will jump off a barn roof with a bed sheet imagining it will work as a parachute and break their legs. They have barely begun to figure out what is impossible.

Children's minds are just beginning to detect that contradictory claims can't both be true. For the first time they begin checking to see if parents are telling them the truth. They no longer believe everything they are told. Their minds can now understand negative instructions and decode negative statements like "Don't run," to mean "Stop yourself from running" instead of "STOP and RUN."

---

[1] From Erik Erikson's developmental stages.

Doing hard things. At five, children develop the capacity to do things that they don't feel like doing. This is the first they realize that other people don't always do what they feel like doing. From this, children develop the ability to do hard things. Hard things are things that they don't feel like doing but choose to do anyway. This capacity begins to emerge at five and must be strengthened and developed over the next seven years to be ready for adulthood.

Hiking up a mountain can be a hard thing to do. There is a ridge below the five Cottonwood lakes that are home to the rare golden trout. Jamie and several others had an introduction to hard things along its endless switchbacks. Their backpack grew heavier with each step. Air was thin at 10,800 feet and all the children were panting and standing far more than they were walking. The more they stood, the stiffer they got and the harder it was to walk. "How much farther is it?" gave way to hot tears and cries of:

"I can't go!"

"I can't walk any more!"

"I can't move!"

"I want to go home!"

Their moaning was clear proof that we had exceeded their storehouse of joy. A return to Joy Camp was the only goal left. The problem was that our Joy Camp destination was still uphill. Fifty feet below the top of the ridge but before we could see it, we passed two men coming down.

"How much farther to the top?" one boy asked.

"Oh! You're halfway there!" the older man said.

Three boys just sat down and cried. They would not talk or move. Their control centers desynchronized. It was only with great encouragement that they started again. They were delighted to discover five minutes later that the men had been wrong. They made it! They did a hard thing!

A flat alpine meadow stretched out the rest of the way to our campsite. I arrived carrying four sleeping bags and Matthew's backpack. Matthew was the youngest child in the group and not ready for something quite as hard as the others. The children who weren't dehydrated returned to joy almost as soon as they reached camp. They climbed every rock and fallen tree. They threw every loose stone into the lake.

On later trips we added drinking more water to the list of hard things to do while hiking. It is a hard thing to drink water when you don't feel like it. The goal of childhood is to take care of oneself but there is a lot for a child to learn.

It is pointless trying to teach children under five to do hard things. Their brains have not developed the capacity. Instead they will become discouraged. Then, when they have matured enough so they could actually succeed, they will feel too hopeless to try. Yet, we all know that infants, who can barely walk, need to do things they don't feel like doing. Until they have developed their wills enough to do hard things we must motivate infants and children by changing the way they feel. Sometimes we help them feel good about things they must do, like, "I'll read you a story when you get in bed." This gives them a positive feeling of anticipation—even when we are only telling them what we would have done anyway. Other times we make children feel more unhappy about avoiding a task than they are about doing it. "You will not get dessert until you finish your asparagus in jalapeno sauce." When they become more unhappy about missing dessert than they are about eating this delicacy they will start to eat—about the same time Iceberg Lake thaws, I would say.

Once there is a strong enough identity at age five to override feelings, children can begin choosing to act against the force of their feelings. It is important to start off slowly with this new skill. Five-year-olds can remind themselves to walk when they want to run, and sit still a while when they want to walk. Most of the real practice comes toward the end of childhood during the junior high years. By then children want a challenge.

Of course, no child will want to do hard things, especially at first. They do not like mowing the grass—especially on a hot day, cleaning their room, learning multiplication tables, doing pull-ups, climbing a ridge, completing a merit badge, working until the job is finished or until quitting time, or not acting at the lowest common denominator with every obnoxious child. Character and strength develop as they learn to be more than they thought they could be.

There are few naturally occurring hard things for children in suburbia. There are no cows to milk, gardens to hoe or even newspaper routes before dawn. There are snowblowers and weed whackers only adults can run. Everything else has remote controls.

One educational theory held that children would naturally learn if they were given good self-esteem and a place to explore the world. That theory doesn't teach children to do hard things they don't feel like doing. Much real learning is hard at first. Mathematics, in particular, requires children to think in ways they have never thought before. They must attempt to do something that at first they are unable to do and which must be done a right way. This is hard. The child who has learned to feel satisfied doing hard things will succeed and try even higher goals—perhaps physics or calculus.

The human brain begins life looking for greater minds to copy – minds that understand and know things that the brain does not yet know. Curiosity (a PFC function) and attachment are the connection to greater minds that help children climb to new heights. Early life engagement with greater minds who are glad to be with them builds the skills children will use to learn hard things.

Discovering what Is real. Five years of age is also when children learn to judge whether their feelings are realistic. Until now they always believed everything they felt. If a child under five feels scared of ponies, words or explanations cannot change his fears. After five children can change their feelings when their understanding changes. Children who have someone they trust to tell them the truth, can begin to correct the times their feelings are based on misperceptions. If they are told something is an "accident" they can then go back and begin erasing the offended feeling.

Children who do not have parents they trust to tell them the truth will continue believing their feeling instead of what they are told. They will reject explanations and trust their own feelings to tell them the real truth. If they feel it, it is true. If they feel hurt then you hurt them—even if you intended no such thing.

From six to twelve children are what they learn.[1] This is a process of imagining, testing what is imagined against reality and learning from the results. This process produces many failures and many comparisons. Children depend on their parents to tell them the meaning of these comparisons, failures and successes. As a result children learn to separate and correct what they feel from what they imagine and what is real.

Developing their identity. During this learning time children must learn to see themselves through the eyes of heaven. It is not enough to be seen that way by others. Children begin recognizing their own identities and helping themselves grow. Forming a healthy identity is the most important part of the learning to take care of oneself.

Because each child's identity is a little different from everyone else, they learn to make themselves understandable to others. Asking for what they need instead of waiting for others to guess is another element

---

[1] From Erik Erikson's stages.

of self-care. Instead of withdrawing when they are misunderstood, children verbalize thoughts, feelings, motives and desires to others. Self-expression through words and actions is shaped to reflect each child's true identity.

Play and a child's identity. Children practice their identities as they play. It is called play because the outcome is not so serious. In play, children try out their ideas of how to participate in life. A child with a poorly built identity can learn to manage while playing but might collapse under real-life strain. Children need to play so that they build skills and a wider variety of responses. There is always a trade-off between building a skill and exploring many options. Thus early practice should include essential skills that are needed by adults while being fun at the same time.

Play often includes elements of preparation for future tasks. Kittens play in mock fights preparing for territorial disputes later on in life. They practice pouncing and stalking each other in preparation for hunting. Kittens lick each other in preparation for becoming mothers. Little boys also prepare to become men with their play. They watch super heroes on TV in order to be a hero when they grow up. In some parts of the world they shoot at melons with their bows and arrows to hone their hunting skills. Play is part of identity specialization that builds speed, competence and capacity into the brain's fast white matter.

The best arena for practicing being a father is in being a brother and a friend to others. The best way to practice being a mother is also as a sister and friend. Since it is playtime, these roles are not clearly defined. That is to say, a brother or sister can practice being mothers, fathers or friends. The children are merely learning how people think and engage.

You cannot spend much time around little children without discovering that "fairness" is a big deal. While some writers think it is a bad thing that boys typically spend just as much time arguing about the rules as playing the game, I believe that both are essential to play. Arguing is playing at the adult's role of making things fair for all sides. Adults do this by ensuring that everyone is satisfied including themselves. Children will seek to satisfy themselves if they are mature. If they work things out with each other, they all might even end up back in Joy Camp!

People who dislike this kind of play want everything to be harmonious. If we judge by how much fairness children achieve with their arguments, then we must agree with the critics. In actuality, this type of play usually comes as far from producing fairness as shooting little play arrows into green melons is from hunting wild boar. But play is play. It should not be measured by the same yardstick adults use.

Without the active intervention of adults to help children achieve an adult sense of fairness and history, children may turn fairness issues into control fights over rules as they grow older. If children learn about satisfaction they will soon find control dissatisfying. No one gets to Joy Camp that way. But during play, children can practice and learn fairness with their friends and siblings.

One way we helped our two sons Jamie and Rami prepare for fairness was to make it a family rule that they must work out conflicts between themselves. Even though Jamie was four at the time and Rami was only two, working things out was their job. We informed them of the simple ground rules. If they brought a dispute to our attention or requested our intervention, they were told to sit at a table, and neither one could get up until the other one gave them permission.

Sometimes negotiations were very loud and other times silent. The longest session was close to two hours, as I recall. Did they achieve fairness? I never checked so I don't know, they were just preparing. It did not take long for them, however, to realize the value of mutually satisfying solutions. On one occasion they were simply not able to solve the problem without adult help and both agreed to find that help together. Adult intervention is key at times when real fairness is needed. We will talk more about teaching fairness in book two *Growing Us: becoming an adult.*

Children are asked at times to go beyond fairness and care for their brothers and sisters because the need is there, even if it is not fair at the moment. This means doing a hard thing in order to be satisfied. In this way being a sibling can also prepare a child to be a parent. Provided that the practice is not too intensive and draining, most children will find it gratifying. As with piano lessons, too much of a good thing will kill anyone's interest. Lack of encouragement will also destroy a child's interest in difficult tasks. In addition, there is quite a range of responses between children. Some respond well, others say they will never play the piano or take care of anyone again. Opportunities do not guarantee success.

Out of all the options open to children each child must learn what satisfies. He learns what is just like him, what fits her identity, what expresses who he is in his heart. She learns to apply what heaven sees in her to the life she lives.

A child learns satisfaction. By the time a child reaches twelve years of age, they should be very fluent in saying what they feel and knowing what they need. They should be able to take in everything the world has to offer that is good and reject the bad. Children should know how to be satisfied.

Finding satisfaction is a very important job. It takes a while to learn how to do this well. Incredible as it seems infants will drink gasoline, drain cleaner, and many others things that older children will spit out instantly, recognizing that gasoline will not quench their thirst. When it comes to high sugar drinks, food additives, calories and chemicals, children do not always learn what satisfies as quickly. Adults and care givers often give children pleasure foods as rewards rather than teaching them what satisfies. Without knowing what satisfies, adults will not be able to meet their own needs. While finding out what they should drink is part of what a young child must learn, each year the problems become more complex. A long and difficult climb is needed to reach an understanding of a child's needs and how to satisfy them.

One sunny afternoon my sons discovered some facts about satisfaction. The lesson came from a ladder they found in the garage. With this new toy, they could climb on the garage roof and see all around. Once, when Rami was on the roof he instructed Jamie, who was still on the ground, to help him get down. Jamie simply pushed the ladder away from the roof, giving his brother a quick ride to the ground. Rami's feelings told him instantly that was not the way to meet his need in the future. Fast results were not the most satisfying.

As a twelve-year-old, one of my sons faced a teacher that was very unfair and controlling. This made the boy quite angry on a regular basis. Expressing his anger directly to the teacher was not allowed, so he decided to escape the teacher's control by not doing any of his homework. This also provided a kind of revenge, because not doing homework drove the teacher wild. She would explode each time the assignments were missing. This solution helped my son express his anger indirectly but did not meet his need to learn. Unlike declining gasoline in favor of water, this conflict of needs and feelings proved harder to untangle.

By the time children reach twelve, they should have learned to be satisfied, and that dissatisfaction is not so bad because it is temporary. The satisfied child knows how to meet needs and can choose between competing solutions.

Tragically, the majority of men do not appear to have finished the job of being a boy. Most of us do not know what we feel or how to meet our needs. This leaves us very vulnerable. When we are dissatisfied and do not know what satisfies us we are sitting ducks for anyone who claims to have an answer. Since many women also fail to reach adult maturity they also tend to have problems separating what will satisfy from what will only please.

Advertising, for example, is the fine art of creating dissatisfaction. Advertising is designed to create a feeling of dissatisfaction and then tell us what will meet that need. If adults knew what they felt and what met their needs, advertising would have no impact. There would be no use for advertising except to tell us the price. The popularity of advertising, and the way most people succumb to it, tells me that adults have not finished the child stage and do not know what they feel or need. Being children is simply our time to learn what really satisfies. We will need this skill in every later stage of our lives.

Seeing in myself what God sees. Seeing infants as God sees them certainly prepares them to be children who see in themselves what God sees. This would be a good place to remember that one stage of maturity does not replace the previous stage but rather adds a whole new set of needs and tasks on top of the previous stage. We always need others to see us as God sees us. However, children must now learn to be responsible for seeing themselves as God sees them. Self-examination and self-exploration lead to self-understanding when done with God's company, commentary and guidance. This will seem like a mystery to those who have never stopped to be aware of the thoughts God places in our minds or the sense of shalom (the sense harmony when everything fits together) that follows our noticing God thoughts. However, when we are feeling grateful or appreciative we are more likely to notice these meaningful thoughts. Children need daily practice seeing what God sees in them and around them. Half the time this involves seeing themselves as God does and the rest of the time, seeing others as God does.

Part of exploring the world during childhood includes exploring the spiritual world. During the infant stage most children readily see spiritual things and hear God easily. However, at the beginning of the child stage children begin sorting out their own feelings and fantasies and require some help separating what God wants them to know from what they want to hear. "Jesus says I can have my sister's piece of cake!" should arouse some suspicion in our minds that our five-year-old has some kind of fantasy Jesus going. When one of us hears from God, all those around who hear from God should also feel shalom.

Living in grace. We can summarize the child stage as learning to live in grace. Grace is received as an infant and lets us know we are special without performance. Children learn about performance and work to perform well as an expression of grace. Working to express what is special about us takes a lot of effort and is not easy to achieve. But what is special about us cannot be based on results.

What is special about children is based on the pleasure that God, child, family, friends and community share watching the child grow. During the child stage the child learns to become the custodian of this grace. Ultimately, judging what is satisfying is an expression of grace. We are most satisfied by those relationships, experiences, efforts and activities that grow the special person we are intended to become.

By the end of the child stage each child has become experienced at finding and maintaining their grace – what makes that child special. A child is now ready for the adult stage where there is mutual responsibility for my grace and yours. However, for this to work a child needs to have important needs met.

A CHILD'S NEEDS

Children must have many resources provided for them that they don't even know they need. Without this provision their identities become dehydrated and they don't know it. Sure they may be angry, withdrawn, lethargic, unmotivated, bored or agitated but they have no idea what is missing from their lives. They can hurt themselves or their grades and not know why.

I often use scuba diving to get myself in shape during the winter so that I can go backpacking in the summer. After feeling so sick from dehydration the first backpacking trip I was even more determined to stay strong and healthy. That winter I took myself on a three-day dive trip to the Channel Islands on a live-aboard dive boat. I had been having trouble "clearing" or equalizing the pressure in my ears along with having a stuffy nose on my last few dives so I took along nasal spray and decongestants. During the trip the congestion got worse each day.

On the last day I wondered if I should dive at all. We were going to swim into a beach that was a rookery for sea lions so I overcame my misgivings and dove anyway. My right ear wouldn't clear and I damaged an eardrum. It took a year for my ear to heal before I could dive again. Hundreds of dollars in medical expenses later, my doctor prescribed heavy dosages of decongestants before and during all my dives.

The next summer I was determined to avoid dehydration in the High Sierra by watching when my fingers started swelling and drinking water right away. I wanted to catch the problem well before the nausea started. The first day on the trail I noticed that just before my fingers started to swell my ears would block. Swelling in the nasal tissues around the Eustachian tube that connects the ear and the throat blocked the airflow to my middle ear. As soon as I drank water my ears cleared up. If I waited a little longer before drinking water, my nose got stuffy. It too would clear up when my body had enough water.

In moderately cold water, scuba divers keep themselves warm with wetsuits. It's a bit crude I suppose, but have you ever noticed that when you get cold you need to go to the bathroom more often? A hiker can find a tree but there are no such facilities under water so you can guess what scuba divers do when in need. That is why no one wants to rent a used wetsuit.

My first Christmas after I started diving I bought a beautiful blue wetsuit of my own. In order to keep it clean I cut down on how much coffee I drank before diving. It was after that the problems clearing my ears and sinuses began. On my three-day boat trip I drank as little as possible. Here was my old nemesis *dehydration* again, and under water no less!

Who would think they would get dehydrated under water? Who would guess dehydration would cause stuffy nose, plugged ears leading to damaged eardrums? Who would think dehydration could cause a lack of thirst, loss of appetite leading to lack of energy. Likewise, children who do not know how to act like themselves will show a wide variety of seemingly unrelated symptoms. The same is true for unfinished childhood tasks and needs that remain unmet. The most common of these unrecognized needs for children are: unearned love, a sense of family history, the history of God's family, and a big picture of life.

Children need love they do not earn. Babies often receive lots of freely given love. Children also need love that has no performance requirements. A child needs love that is given because someone knows they are worth it. The need to receive love is with us all of our lives. We call this freely given love—grace. Grace is how we learn about our intrinsic value. The first twelve years of life are the time to learn how to receive. These years establish our value.

All of us have value because we were created with God's life in us. We have value because God values us. It is not because of anything we have done. As babies we should all have the opportunity to learn our intrinsic value otherwise we will think our value comes from what we do. By the time we are two we need to know we have great value without having to do anything at all.

From two until four years-of-age our identities become "I am what I do" so it is hard to know if "doing" is what gives us value or not. Children must continue receiving love that isn't earned throughout the child years so they can be clear that *doing* is good but our value comes from *being*.

A moment of self-examination will cause most men to discover that they believe their value comes from what they can do. If a man can't earn a living, talk and think straight, if he can't contribute to his family or society, he thinks he has lost his value. Boys who don't receive grace become men who turn to achievements, fame, and fortune in order to find value. This is how a four year old thinks. If they must *do* something to feel worth, then men do not know who they really are.

Women continue to be told their value comes from how they look. Women are also told they would have more value by giving pleasure, having babies, providing services or career performance. It seems progressive to let women find their value from what they do. Performance, accomplishment and accumulation should not be rewarded differently for men and women but deriving our value from these things is no better for women than it has been for men.

No culture is going to tell us correctly who we really are. God tells us we have great value for just being made in God's image, so it is only if we look at ourselves from God's point of view that we realize we have great value even if we can't do anything at all.

Becoming protectors. Little girls and boys can be extremely predatory with each other. Children often attack each other's flaws. Hate begins to appear and grow during childhood. Grade school and middle school give rise to bullies. Social media has only increased the reach of predatory children.

Children need coaching and examples on how to notice the weaknesses in others and respond in a protective way. When faced with someone who does not like us or is simply different from us, children need protective examples. Good examples begin by sharing the pain that others feel because shared pain helps us find and implement the least harmful solutions to problems. Shared pain helps the brain's fast track identity processing escape from seeing others as enemies.

Children develop protective identities in many ways. Protecting books, equipment, household goods, plants, animals, nature, ecosystems, environment, quiet, diet, family, friends, neighbors, babies, private parts of our body, our health, our work, family finances, God's work and our neighborhood will each require awareness, examples and encouragement.

Family history. As children near twelve they need to be taught the family history. Family history illustrates to children how well people they know have taken care of themselves and others. Have they shared pain, been protective, matured or failed to mature? What has happened as a result over the next several generations? The only history children readily understand is that of their own family. Learning from known examples illustrates how their responsible and irresponsible actions impact others.

Training a child between nine and twelve in family history is easy— just tell stories. Family story telling is a big part of developing a well-balanced brain. During these last years of childhood their interest in parents is at its height. Children are beginning to study what they will be like as adults and they really want to know how parents think and live. Just before junior high is perhaps the best time to teach them how the world of relationships works. Soon the crude social power-plays of junior high will cloud their ability to see positive ways people can impact each other.

Tales of the guardians of life. The history of God's family sounds like religion to most people and it turns them off. Suppose with me that God is life. God is what it means to be fully alive and God is passionate that life be full and good. Would the guardian of life not give guidelines for living? Would Life not want people to study and know the ways of life and avoid the ways that lead to death?

Children need to know more than their family history if they are to grow up as people who are alive and life-giving. For their growth and understanding, children must hear the stories of the people of God— the people who lived and brought life. They need to know life so they will not join gangs that kill, cheat on their husbands, beat their wives and children, pour contempt on those they love and fail to learn about the source of life and goodness. History and movies are full of these themes and yet until a child realizes that life has a history and heritage in real men and women who made sometimes difficult choices so life could go on, they will not be ready to become adults.

The big picture. Childhood is also the time to learn the "big picture" of life. This means knowing the stages and goals for each of the five stages of life, much as they were described in chapter one. People really need a map. It is amazing how much struggle this removes from teen years and the later stages of life. Children who know where they are going will fight their parents far less than those who are just being pushed along without knowing the goal.

During late childhood children can understand goals and are happy pursuing the same goals as their parents. By ten or twelve they can understand how each stage of life builds on the previous stage. Children appreciate complexity and they are already becoming complex themselves. It is a good time to help them understand how your family has handled the transition to adult life. Your child will stay your ally more easily since you have prepared them to grow up. I have written an entire book on this subject entitled *Rite of Passage.*[1]

When I taught my younger son Rami to drive we took the complex process in stages. First, he worked on the accelerator then the clutch and the brake. My head shook back and forth like a maraca in a Tijuana band while he learned how to use the brakes. When Rami began combining the controls, he would forget what he had learned about the accelerator when he used the clutch. When we added steering, he almost forgot about the clutch. In time, we added driving in traffic to the tasks and thankfully he remembered the previous steps. His speed and capacity to accomplish the central driving skills developed. So it is with growing up, each stage builds on the previous ones. Knowing the big picture helps us fit it all together and look forward to what is next.

PEERS BEFORE PUBERTY

In *Girls on the Brink*, neuroscience author Donna Jackson Nakazawa states that we have "stolen girl's safe in-between years."[2] Nakazawa, also the author of *Childhood Disrupted*, states, "Anyone caring for girls today knows that our daughters, students, and girls next door are more anxious and more prone to depression and self-harming than ever before."[3]

---

[1] E. James Wilder, Rite of Passage (Ann Arbor: Servant Publications, 1994.)
[2] Donna Nakazawa, Girls on the Brink, (New York: Harmony 2022) p. 36.
[3] Ibid inside cover.

The years from nine to thirteen (middle school grades five and six) were sheltered years of friendship and mutual support within gender groups. Boys practiced being themselves with other boys. Girls practiced with other girls. The effect of removing the safe zone to play practice child identities with peers has produced performance based identity and anxiety. There is no safe way to become ME and practice before my body, looks, performance and desirability determine my worth.

Peers before puberty have, for generations, been primarily same gender peers. Becoming ME and practicing my gender's specialties (with as many major consequences removed as possible) has been the safe zone of childhood. Not only has the safe zone disappeared but demands that children be good at everything has taken its place. Even worse, some feel the expectation that they must be better than other children. Immature parents strongly contribute to this crisis by selectively favoring their child. "We live in a "my kid first," "anti-tribe" era,"[1] Nakazawa says.

After adding early sexualization to the list of damaging factors, Nakazawa points out that the child's brain is not prepared for these pressures and resulting comparisons that produce competition for value.

But, if childhood is to be a safe zone to learn how to take care of oneself, risks must be introduced at the speed the child is ready to handle. This attunement to the child's capacity creates a tension between keeping the child safe and taking meaningful risks. Historically, mothers monitored safety while fathers introduced the small risks that helped children grow. However the virtual "reality" of cyberspace has proven very hard to monitor and produced one of the least sheltered environments in a child's life.

In the next chapter we will look at how the father guides and participates in his children's childhood. Dads really come into their own during the childhood years. These years can be very satisfying when you remember to drink enough water and take care of whatever you need.

---

[1] Ibid p. 41.

Chapter Eight
Children and Fathers

The child grew and was weaned, and [on the day of his weaning] Abraham gave a great feast. Genesis 21:8

I was four the first time my dad took me blueberry picking. Grandpa Jacobson and Uncle August kept track of forest fires because burnt out areas would have great blueberry crops the next few years. Grandpa and his brother both sported gray beards and spoke very little. They climbed in our pastel-green 1955 Plymouth station wagon next to our family of four and we headed for a burnt out section of land near Baudette.

It was a blueberry extravaganza. The old men picked quarts of berries. I picked about what I ate. It was amazing to walk, pick and eat. I was living off the land!

Baudette was a three hundred and twenty mile round trip for my dad who kept track of mileage very carefully. His one-year-old Plymouth was the economy version with no oil filter and Dad was serious about regular oil changes. I was learning to take care of my things.

Each adventure with Dad started with leaving home and ended with a return to rest. I learned that both leaving and returning are good. Disconnecting and connecting again formed an endless succession and a life rhythm. The world was for exploration and an adventure to enjoy. Dad made sure it was safe enough but still a chance to stretch and grow.

Children set out to see who they can be today. As soon as children learn how it is done they launch their own adventures in the care of their watchful community, for their community has been prepared by their father to receive them.

This process is a stress on father, just as teaching the child to ask for his needs was a stress to his mother. The father's desire to see his child

grow provides the motivation to overcome this strain. Fathers who train
their children out of fear push them to perform and achieve rather than
teaching them to explore, express themselves, and find satisfaction in
life.

Through this maze of confusion, it is the father who guides his
children to satisfaction. When you are living off the land, the choices
are not all good. Does a child choose chocolate chip cookies or broccoli,
potatoes or zucchini, eggs or liver, wine or cola? What should we eat
first? When should we not eat?

Learning about food is just the beginning of choosing between
options. What clothes should we wear, what friends should we choose,
what activities should we spend our play time doing? What goals are
worth effort, suffering or pain to obtain? What should be turned down
even if it is immediately pleasurable because it is not satisfying? Father is
the one who, through finding out what really satisfies in life, can guide
his child's steps and choices. In time, father will show his children the
difference between pleasure and satisfaction, and in so doing the
children will learn wisdom.

Does a father teach his children to live in the world and care for the
land because a mother can't? Not in the slightest! But it is particularly
redemptive for men when they do. Teaching children to be explorers
and protectors is something that men and boys need to practice
regularly if they are to tame their inner predators. Track, find, chase,
enjoy, share and protect are central to living off the land for generation
after generation.

FATHERS SYNCHRONIZE WITH CHILDREN

We have said a lot about synchronizing with babies. First the parent
must synchronize to the baby but after nine months the baby can begin
to synchronize to the parent—within limits. As children get older those
limits need to keep stretching. Dad needs to keep close track of all
progress. A positive father will measure progress by the child while a
negative father will measure progress by the goal. A negative father says,
*"You are still leaving your room a mess. I told you I wanted everything
picked up"* A positive father will say, *"I see you are picking up your clothes
now. What are you going to pick up next?"*

The biggest part of growing up is not about the work you do but
about how you handle your feelings and impulses. The baby had to
learn how to feel joy and all the unpleasant emotions as well, but the

child must take on the urgent drives linked to survival. Babies cannot overcome anything that seems to threaten their survival but children need to master even these feelings so they will not become tyrants. While both boys or girls need this training boys must become specialists. Boys must be taught these dad skills or the next generation will not be safe around young males. Obviously there isn't a lot of that going on.

Perhaps it would be a good time to remember that there is no need for specialization if our goal is not building a multigenerational community of joy and peace. Men and women do not need to be specialized if they only take care of themselves as apex predators. But staying joyfully attached for a lifetime and raising children who can do the same has always meant some specialization.

It isn't going to kill you. This conflict between two necessary forces—safe limits and new growth—often has parents split. If mother's favorite phrase was, "Be careful," Dad's is, "It won't kill you." Dads seem to intuitively know that we need to learn to distinguish what will really kill us from what only feels that way. Can you hear dad say, "It isn't going to kill her to: Stay up late, jump in the pool, wait to eat, do something she doesn't want to do, have ice cream before salad or fall off her bike?"

While sometimes the battle is between dad and mom, other times it is between parents and child. Children need to learn to delay gratification and do hard things they don't feel like doing. Not only will it not kill them to suffer these discomforts, but failing to delay gratification or do hard things can prove to be life threatening under the wrong circumstances. We looked at doing hard things in the previous chapter so let's look at cravings that must be resisted.

The beast each child must tame is the feeling that roars, "You are killing me" when they can't get what they want. As a baby, both parents would help her or him calm down when she couldn't get what she wanted. As an infant his parents stopped him from getting things he craved but should not have. Now that they are children, Dad must teach them how to tame a brain that screams, "I'll die if I don't get it!"

Dad says, "It isn't going to kill you" but then must show children how to live with unfulfilled desires. Children are not too sure they won't die because the intense signal they are listening to is coming from the brain's survival center in the limbic system. Yet, if they can't control cravings now they will really have trouble when adolescent hormones kick in to amplify their urges and desires.

Deep in each brain the *nucleus accumbens* creates overpowering urges for bonding, food, safety and eventually sex. Because these are strong survival "drives" our brain makes their voices intense and urgent. We feel as though we will not live if we don't fill these desires. Learning to tame these intense signals is a job that falls largely on Dad. Now, you will no doubt have noticed that a great number of men have had no success dealing with their appetites, urges, impulses and drives. They will, of course be useless in training their child since they have not learned control themselves. People once said that a bit of religion would do those men some good.

The nucleus accumbens is such a strong factor in life that most great religions contain teaching about how to train and restrain these drives. Among the Jewish and Christian stories, we read about Esau who lost his birthright to Jacob because Esau thought he would die if he didn't get some lentil stew. Denying all cravings and attachments is central to Buddhist training. For Buddhists, the brain that has not mastered its desires is like a wild monkey. Jesus spent forty days fasting before he began to teach in order to ensure that he would not make his own survival his priority. He had to tame his survival circuits. Muslims practice fasting one month a year. Sexual abstinence is central to the Catholic Church priesthood and those priests who have not tamed their nucleus accumbens have brought numerous crises to the church. Learning higher values than our own survival and learning to direct cravings to God are all part of the spiritual disciplines in the Christian tradition.

The nucleus accumbens not only responds to our survival drives like attachments, food, safety and sex but it is also the part of our brains that reacts to cocaine, heroin, alcohol, nicotine, caffeine, ecstasy, "speed," and other drugs. It is closely tied to the cravings that make those drugs addictive. Training the mind to handle this powerful center that screams, "I'll just die if I don't get it," is a crucial part of avoiding addictions.

When teen years come, sexual hormones (testosterone and estrogen) will make the nucleus even more sensitive and reactive. Its training begins when baby screams as though he would die because he wants Mommy and he has Daddy instead. Dad's presence, closeness and reassurance while he screams as though he would die is the first reassurance that the nucleus is not always right. Of course the dad who has not tamed his own nucleus will be chasing Bathsheba, downloading porn, having a toke, watching TV, playing video games, obsessed with work or eating and drinking. Everyone needs nucleus accumbens control but boys should specialize if they want to be trainers for the next generation.

Controlling urges involves learning to survive their siren song as well as learning how to control the brain circuits that set off the alarm. To keep the nucleus from getting in a spasm we must be good at producing joy and bringing ourselves to calm—surprise!

You can see which one of these two (joy or calm) people have trouble with by looking at the addictions they chose. Addictions typically involve a stimulant for those who do not know how to produce joy on their own or a depressant (like alcohol) for those who do not know how to produce peace on their own. We can crave being alive (stimulants like cocaine) just as we crave becoming calm (narcotics and food.)

Let me tell you a story. As we have already begun to see, stories help greatly to synchronize the left and right sides of the child's brain during the childhood stage of development. Dads have a special part of this means of synchronization. Children over four now have the two sides of their brains connected so they can really benefit from mutual story telling about the emotional events of the day. *"Tell me what happened at school today,"* is an important part of family interactions. Even that simple skill is built learning to, *"Tell Mommy what we did today,"* as well as listening to Daddy tell the stories of his day. Dads who develop the skill can become very good at telling stories of family adventures and misadventures. In fact, telling truthful, authentic, accurate and complete stories about misadventures and negative feelings helps calm the mind and build peace. A well-trained mind can produce joy when needed and calm itself when needed by remembering stories.

I discovered the power of family stories when I worked at a counseling center that saw over over a thousand appointments a month—primarily with women who had been sexually abused. Many of these women hated men. Many of the men they hated were their husbands. I developed a reputation as a miracle worker with their husbands by changing most of them into wonderful guys in only three visits. The men were never to divulge to their wives what I told them to do, but here it is:

1. When you get home each day tell your wife three stories about your day. These stories must involve people you saw or interacted with during that day.

2. Before you can brush your teeth for bed you must tell three
    stories of us. Go through old picture albums to find them if
    you can't remember any.
3. Get a good storybook and read your wife a story or chapter
    each night when you get in bed. This helps end the day in joy
    and since so many sexually abused women didn't have good
    childhoods or bedtimes it builds good memories to replace bad.

The only other thing I did in those three visits was to explain the
nature of treatment and recovery to the men. No one had ever told
them what to expect. Men do much better when they know what is
going on. In under two weeks the men went from the bottom of the
barrel to the top. Soon the women's groups would sponsor three visits
with me for particularly "hopeless" men. The results were the same.

Of course every woman guessed the storybook at bedtime was my
idea, they just couldn't guess how I got the "bum" to do it. They did not
guess the nature of the real change in his story telling.

The reason I made my instructions secret is that abused women
have trouble understanding that men can love intentionally as well as
spontaneously. Due to damage in their maturity process, particularly
learning from trustworthy people that feelings are not always right, the
women would have discounted intentional love even though it was real.

Singing songs does much the same as story telling. Dads who sing
and tell stories, help their children to harmonize the way they think and
feel. Singing over your children when they are falling asleep or making
up silly songs about them builds joy.

MORE USES FOR FATHERS

When I think back on my story of becoming a father, I remember
eating my stack of blueberry pancakes the day my first child was born.
That day I could not think of any uses for fathers. Feeling useless as a
dad can become a self-fulfilling prophesy, but with desire there is hope.
We have not nearly tapped the power of the father-child bond.[1] It is the
main motive for men to mature.

Cooperation skills Children learn how to cooperate from joining
the teamwork between their parents. The obvious joy and peace parents
achieve through helping each other, motivates children to work and play
cooperatively as well.

---

[1] Dr. Ken Canfield at the National Center for Fathering. www.fathers.com 1(800) 593-DADS

Three-way bonds allow for flexible and helpful interactions between three or more people. Dad is a crucial part of children's brain development when it comes to three way interactions. Even in families with lots of siblings, the modeling flows from the top down. Few children can work together as smoothly and joyfully as mature adult parents. If dad and mom possess well-trained, mature brains it will be second nature for them to work together. If one or both parents have an ignorant or untrained brain life is going to be tense.

Evaluating children's efforts Children learn much from their mothers and fathers, but they practice what they learn with their siblings and peers. As you would expect, they compare lessons with each other as well as practicing on each other. The influence of these practice sessions is considerable in every child's development. Parents who supervise these practice sessions will find that helping their children evaluate the results strengthens the lessons they want to teach. Unexamined or unregulated play can often teach children very different lessons about who they are or what they can do. The good father is attentive to this possibility and reviews what his children are learning from life experiences be sure the conclusions are satisfying.

Group participation T-ball, soccer, little league, Scouts, camping, band, church and all aspects of becoming a child will eventually require participation in a group. The skills children learn interacting with parents and siblings are a big part of their social intelligence. What determines their place in the social pecking order, however, is the motivation they learn to use. Motives will always be either fears or desires. A well-trained control center builds children who run on desire.

A father whose pride and joy rolls out the red carpet for his daughter or son's entrance into the community removes a child's fears and strengthens healthy desires. The child arrives on the other side of this metamorphosis ready to learn and grow. Abraham, as you recall, held a feast to introduce his son when Isaac was weaned. His father became his advocate, defender, encourager and interpreter in their community.

Tag team fathering No child with only one father has enough fathers. Because each father has his own limitations, a father's duty is to secure additional fathers for his children. Males, who need a little more redemption, especially need more than one father. Men's identities have got some things missing and most are stuck at infant maturity. Incomplete development leaves men with identities like

Swiss cheese. This and several other reasons suggest a need for supplementing male development for the next generation.

First, just like stacking many slices of Swiss cheese will cover the holes, having many models of mature men will raise a boy with fewer holes in his identity. By adding additional fathers, a dad raises his son to become someone greater than himself. By taking in the diversity of different men's fathering abilities, a boy will grow past his father's limitations and blind spots much more readily.

Second, the boy with many fathers learns early in life about the presence and power of the spiritual family. His world is larger, his vision and opportunities are multiplied, and he has much more life to see, explore and receive. He can find an experienced guide for every mountain he wants to climb, every skill he wants to learn.

Third, the boy with many fathers is much safer in times of trouble. Should his father be gone, injured, or die he will have other men in his life. When his parents are overwhelmed there will be places to turn. Should a phase of life be particularly rough at home, like adolescence, he will have mature support to see him through the difficult terrain.

Fourth, the boy with many fathers will be better prepared for future growth and maturity. He will move more easily into his community after weaning and enter the community of men smoothly when he becomes a man. He will even find it more natural to find and receive help from other fathers when he becomes a dad. This support from other fathers is the single most important human factor in becoming a better father.[1]

Fifth, multiple fathers help raise hopeful girls. When the men in and around the home are "working on their stuff," learning to be relational with everyone, seeing each woman and child through the eyes of heaven, teaching their inner predators to become protectors (as we will examine in the next book in this series), it builds joy and hope in a girl's heart.

So why have I put so much emphasis on boys? Because, during my professional lifetime I found that three fourths of girls successfully made it through the first metamorphosis into child maturity when only one fourth of boys did so. That indicates to me that we have been doing a much better job with girls. But, we can do better with at least a fourth of girls as well.

If the necessary training is not being done with boys it must be deliberately reintroduced. If most men have maturity gaps then it

---

[1] Dr. Ken Canfield.

will take a cluster of them working together to represent what maturity is like. Further, since infant maturity requires fitting the lesson to the infant, then infant maturity men need men as models. If three fourths of men have grown up with totally inadequate training we can be sure that they will not be adequate models. After a while we start thinking this is how men are. Growing a more human community means aiming higher.

DEFECTIVE BONDS WITH FATHER

I have known and had relationships with people born in the late 1800s through Generation Alpha and the rates of maturity in men are always lower than in women. This is not a new problem and it repeats from one generation to the next. Men are generally less mature than women. Something now seems to be equalizing the ratio by lowering the maturity levels in women to match the immaturity levels in men. Meanwhile, people are foolishly trying to encourage women to be more like men as a way to create equality.

My brother Tim was the first to point out to me that the Bible narrative consistently points to men having more trouble being who they were created to be. It started the moment that Adam ate the fruit. My friend Ed Khouri uses the phrase, "Men need more redemption" to address the problem. While this is not the place to discuss the theology (although some men get their knickers in a knot about it) men need more remediation. Because identity is built through attachments, a critical failure happens between fathers and sons.

We can better understand the importance of a boy's bonds with his father when we look at what happens if they are missing or defective. Having no bond to his father leaves the boy adrift within himself and adrift in the world of men. The man who is unconnected with his father does not trust other men. He does not trust his wife or daughter with other men either.

Weak bonds. The man who is not connected with his father is at great risk of becoming a conformist. He does not know how to be separate and make things happen. He is more prone to be changed than to cause changes. He is not in full possession of his own capacity. This makes it hard to do what needs doing. Dad is the one who teaches us to go after what we want and make things happen.

A weak bond with Dad produces a frantic search for control, power and freedom. Such men need to get away from what they fear will control them. This kind of man fears commitment, challenge, work and struggle. It doesn't matter who gets hurt as he tries to escape. Rather than the connection to his father that tells him he can stay relational and make things happen, there is fear which leads to running away. Escape is necessary when strength is missing—strength to get involved and stay involved. Men run away to work, sports, and study. Some have made minor careers out of trying to be free of any responsibilities in life.

God when portrayed as our Father says, "When you have done everything, stand." Men who know this kind of God don't need to run. God promises the strength needed to stay even when we might suffer. We can go, we can do, we can be what is needed but we don't need to run. There is no frantic search for freedom. Jesus did not run around saying, "Let me out of here, these people are trying to run my life."

I get afraid to stay involved sometimes so I run away. I remember one time a family fight broke out on an old subject – eating salad actually. Meals frequently included this fight. I quickly decided to go to the back bedroom to pray. It was the perfect cover. I would gladly have prayed until everything was better, and I could go back out safely. God didn't like my using Him to escape my responsibility so instead of peace, my pious escape brought me growing agitation. Before long I had to rejoin the family and take a stand. I don't know that we resolved anything that day, but God knew I could take the heat.

Not only is the missing father a problem, but at times an involved father will fail to be a good model and so create problems by his presence. Each boy is the closest replica on earth of what his father is like. How he feels about his father will have a huge impact on how he sees himself. Even in trying to be very different from his father, the boy is not free from the powerful influence of these feelings.

If a large oak tree drops an acorn that grows into an oak tree, it will be the closest replica of the original oak tree that we can find. Still, the effects of climate, lightning, wind and disease may cause the two trees to grow very differently. In that sense the boy can be the closest replica of who his father was created to be, although through the effects of climate he may grow in very different ways.

God didn't create any trash. We trash ourselves and get trashed because there is evil in the world. But even if your father was the worst father in the world, that is not how his life was supposed to grow. We can say he malfunctioned. Stripped of all the sentimental guilt, human evil is nothing other than a malfunction of identity. To see dad through the eyes of heaven, we see an oak tree that never grew up right. The lightning strike of '37 and the winter of '52 took their toll. The seed of the oak tree need not grow that way.

Broken bonds. If boys or men totally reject their fathers, they reject the model on which they were based. Such a rejection is a rejection of their very selves. Total rejection of parents will trip up our identities. Until each of us can see our fathers through the eyes of heaven and see which parts of Dad are the distortions left by evil and what is the created design, we cannot see ourselves correctly either. For men, this acceptance is crucial.

If someone were in a car accident and went through the windshield, we would NOT assume that what we found in the wreckage was what their face should look like. We can figure that out because we know what faces should look like, but we don't really know what damage has been done to people's souls, especially when we grow up with them. That face we saw on our father we took to be normal. We could not tell what the scars were unless our father was honest about his history. The truth comes from looking at this history through the eyes of heaven.

To look at injured people with understanding we must know what they were before the injury. People with faces full of glass from the windshield will rightfully see themselves as ugly, but are they ugly? First we must take the glass out and stitch up their faces.

To stretch this analogy a bit, all of us have had our faces jammed through the windshield of sin in the world. (Sin is whatever keeps us from acting like ourselves.) We need our faces reconstructed by someone who knows what they should look like to begin with. A plastic surgeon would want a "before" picture. But since our world is thousands of years into the wreck, we have to go back to the Creator for a "before" picture. We can no longer determine whether our faces should look as they do, or if what we see is the result of generations of damage. We ask our Creator to pick the glass out and build our face so that it looks like our father, the way our father was meant to look. In doing this we must come to terms with the fact that our father has also gone through the windshield. His face has also been crushed, and cleaning up his face is God's business, not ours. Often a father has disfigured his son's face to match his own using the same shards of glass. Many a son has undertaken to put glass right back in his father's face to show him what it feels like.

Fear bonds. At one point in my training when I was being instructed in behavior modification, my services were requested to help a boy who was not doing well in school. We set up a program of goals he could reach. In return he received certain rewards. The reward the boy requested was to spend some time with his dad doing something fun. The father agreed and the standards for success were set. The boy began applying himself diligently to his studies and earned all his points.

Two weeks later the family came in again. The boy was worse then ever, so I asked what went wrong. The boy said, "I did everything, but my dad would not spend time with me."

I asked his father if this were true and said, "Hey! That is how the world is! You don't always get what you expect. The kid just has to learn to live with that."

The dad was happy! He had just taught his son a valuable lesson— what it is like to have your face put through the windshield of life. Now his boy's face would look like his father's. This is how he saw being a good father. He needed to teach certain lessons and get the glass arranged in his son's face the way it was in his own. This is what happens when you don't have the eyes of heaven to see what someone ought to look like. As far as I could determine, this father was well intentioned.

Much training is done by those who don't know how a face ought to look. Deep inside, men sense something wrong with the ways they treat their children. And yet, without the courage to face their own pain and their own losses, the trickle-down of cruelty is inevitable. Men, particularly fathers, must face the fact that the mentors, fathers, elders, and role models that they seek are not usually available. For my generation the first and last step of grief has been giving what we never received. It is the first step because unless we give, we will not grieve deeply. It is the last because when we have grieved our losses, we will have life to give.

Suppose that we never reach child maturity and just push on with life? Certainly a lack of preparation will make most life-tasks unsustainable or low joy. Three out of four men of my generation have lived this way along with one in four women. We cannot push on as though we know what we are doing without having our children and grandchildren noticing that we have lost the trail.

A MAN AND HIS FATHER

It makes me uncomfortable to say so, but there have been times when my marriage got a little bumpy. Perhaps you know what I mean. Some bumps have lasted more than a few hours or even a few days. It was on a particularly long bump that I called my dad. He, in his wisdom, reminded me of my original intentions in marrying my wife. Over the phone he took me back to Bemidji Park and our conversation fifteen years before.

I remembered the day that my dad asked me about my desire to get married. In his opinion and that of the state of Minnesota, I was too young. Did I know, he inquired, of the difficulties inherent in my decision? As we walked through the park at the edge of Lake Bemidji and glanced at the paintings by local artists, we reviewed my life—past, present and future.

"You knew there would be tough times when you got married," Dad reminded me. "I seem to recall that you wanted the challenge." He was right. A man sometimes needs his father to help him do hard things. My mind flashed to a childhood cartoon. Dad's challenge reminded me of Superchicken's words to Fred, "You knew the job was dangerous when you took it!"

But my father's compassion was deeper than it appeared at first, and we talked at some length about what it means to do things that strain and even hurt. Though he did not particularly agree with me or support all that I was doing, my dad reminded me of my history, my commitments and, most importantly, that there wasn't anything unmanly about feeling pain. The stories-of-us helped me remember how to act like myself.

A man's connection to his father goes on forever. A wise father will try to bring the best out of us, for he can see with the eyes of heaven what there is inside of us waiting to come out. We do well to return often to such words and remember them.

HOPEFUL GIRLS

Hopeful girls have likely been the main contributors to cultural and economic progress across human history.[1] What has traditionally made girls hopeful is how women and babies are treated. When life for women and babies is painful, girls feel dread. They dread growing up and they dread having babies. Much of this dread comes from how men treat women and babies. Predatory activity by men is high on the list of things that make life painful. Teaching boys to protect women and babies, their mothers, sisters, aunts, neighbor girls along

[1] Lloyd deMause, Childhood and Cultural Evolution, The Journal of Psychohistory, Vol 26, #3, Winter 1999, p. 642-723.

with vulnerable people, becomes an essential part of sustaining hopefulness.

The power and motivation that sustains protectiveness is joy. Learning what makes women and babies really glad to be with us (joy) is what boys need to learn from their fathers. Fathers must exemplify how to build joy with the opposite gender. To build safe and protective attachments with the women of the family and community that contribute to joy (a group of people who are glad to be together) fathers must help boys develop their three-way bonds.

Three-way bonds require attachments to two other people at the same time and that is where having two parents becomes important. The two parents must have a sustained joyful relationship or the child's brain will begin predicting that family attachments will be painful rather than joyful.

Three-way family bonds feature the right dorsolateral prefrontal cortex that is specialized for father attachments. Fathers develop the dorsolateral PFC when they attach to their children during the growth spurt that starts at eighteen months as we saw in chapter four. This same protector system provides our conscience when properly developed. This center for family joy resists the tendency to sexualize after age twelve that happens with two-way bonds in the cingulate cortex. Without learning protectiveness in these three-way bonds they can later be deployed for predatory and sociopathic exploitation of weakness in others. As long as three of four boys continues failing to reach child maturity there will be lots of sexual exploitation. There will be unwanted babies as well.

Developing three-way bonds that produce joy requires huge amounts of practice for boys. Three-way joy bonds require frequent relational involvement by men and fathers. Fathers set the example boys learn from the best. Fathers teach through stories of their own lives. Fathers teach through learning from their own errors. This is how maturity develops in community. This is how communities make room for hopeful girls.

Hopeful girls become hopeful mothers. We will take a brief look at how mothers influence their children across the entire lifespan in our next chapter. They are building a more human community for the generations of the future.

Chapter Nine
Mothers for Life

Kitty and I walked around Budapest trying to learn a few simple words of Hungarian. The language was not easy. Three-year-olds we met chatted as though Hungarian was the world's simplest language. In Korea, the little children were equally at home in their language. Our host's children easily fed themselves glass noodles using metal chopsticks. I could not get the noodles to my mouth. In Sri Lanka and Thailand children ate hot peppers that made my eyes burn just looking at them. These small people had already learned to "be like" their people.

When it came time to have our babies, Kitty wrapped them in a cloth and would "goyo" them African style while her American friends worried that the babies would not be safe on her back. Mothering is learned in the brain's fast track by watching people and storing the examples faster than conscious thought can track the learning. As a result, we are not aware we were learning from our people until we begin acting like them.

A REVIEW OF THE INFANT AND WEANING

What an intimate world surrounds a baby. It is a world made to the best of the parents' ability. It is a place so intimate that we must take our feelings by the hand just to look inside. It is a world of touching and sensing, of knowing and loving, and once in a while, of holding our noses.

Breathing, sleeping, eating, moving, joy and rest all build a strong bond with his mother during his first year of life. Soon he knows that Mother is a person with a mind, too. Her mind knows him, helps him, enjoys him and shares good experiences with him. By synchronizing with Mother's mind he learns to synchronize his own. He climbs Mount Joy, resting when needed.

About the time baby turns one and begins to walk, his mother, the rock of his security, begins to change. This slow, gradual change allows him to experience tiny doses of frustration and disappointment. No longer does she always come at his call. She will not always guess what is wrong. But Mommy keeps an eye on him and before he can plunge over the cliff to despair she helps him to hope. He learns the paths back to Joy Camp.

But as each day goes past the baby learns to ask and receive. He (or she) learns who to ask and how to say it well. "Go ask Daddy to tie your shoes," says Mommy. "Do you want more pureed peas?" or "How's my pumpkin today?" These all herald a passage into a world of words. The baby is preparing to be weaned.

With parents' help the baby will leave infancy behind. Soon he or she will stand on their own. As the end of his third year approaches, he will have developed enough hope to try taking care of himself. These days his mother's words are, "Tell me what you want," or "What is wrong?," or the most dreaded of all, "You'll have to wait until dinner."

Weaning is the end of infancy. Weaning is a huge transition that can only be made by a well-trained four-year-old brain. A mature toddler with a brain capable of self-regulation, synchronization with others and of guiding relationships through both words and feelings is ready for the next step. For many, maybe most four-year-olds, this is not the case. The infant turns four and starts the next stage ill prepared, ignorant and destined to do poorly. Baby's bonds have not prepared them for what is to come. Weaning time is dawning ready or not.

BE-LIKE STUFF RULES

As we saw in chapter two, a baby's brain begins growing be-like areas soon after birth. Be-like regions of the brain become one third of the adult brain and are not present at birth. This giant "copy machine" in the brain is not a passive reference library. This duplication system rules! Secure attachment experiences provide proper training of our be-like stuff that can improve how our DNA is activated creating a stronger influence than genetic predisposition toward depression and addiction. Entering bad examples into the duplicator can activate genetic weaknesses and create problems we could have avoided.

As a culture, we tend to think some conflicted things about genetic tendencies. When genes push us toward allergies, alcoholism, cancer, depression, obesity and baldness we see no problem in battling against genetics. Meanwhile, sexual attraction is only mildly influenced by genetics and we argue about who is "born that way." Gender and sexuality provide significant aspects of our identities. Some aspects are highly controlled by genetics while others are only slightly impacted and greatly formed by be-like influences. Leaving these duplication processes to chance makes little sense. It also makes little sense to think that identities formed through duplication can be changed later by choice. We should not oversimplify complex processes.

Any and all differences in how we value people based on biology are completely unhelpful. Also damaging are judgments that cause toxic shame and arise from a failure to see what God sees and loves in each person.

DNA establishes many of our limits. We will not grow wings or gills even if we try. There are limits to be-like stuff. Kitty 's brother and sister were born in Nigeria. When their family visited the USA friends would ask why the two born in Africa were not black. In short, genetics provides a range of options but be-like material controls a significant amount of how our DNA is expressed. Even immune systems are learning. The brain learns a lot!

DNA must be activated or it lays there dormant. Some DNA must be activated daily. We have far more potential than we can ever activate. Be-like stuff in the brain has DNA that must be activated by the proper stimulation or we will never know it is there. Adults must find, activate and train many capacities. Simply letting children discover themselves is a flawed plan that leaves DNA activation to random experiences. If we stop and think about it, many parents leave a lot of activation and duplication to chance. Infants who are watching screens, going to daycare or home with overly tired parents may be exposed to a thousand experiences that we might not want duplicated and leave valuable characteristics that are not activated properly.

For hundreds of generations of human life we have been developing different strengths in men and women. The advantages of staying with these strengths should be considered. Our biology can provide added strength potential that way. Children can use male and female parents to most advantage when development helps boys duplicate genetically favored male identity strengths and girls the female identity strengths. The same applies to both genders when attempting to grow a heterosexual identity.

The idea that we can easily disregard our DNA is a fantasy. We can only modify male bodies into female and female to male superficially.

Current modifications are destructive and painful. Worse yet, adapting to the modifications burns up developmental time that be-like stuff needs for growth.

DEVELOPMENT HAS DEADLINES

The amazing capacity of the brain to learn and duplicate bigger brains is greatly shaped by critical growth periods and apoptosis. Apoptosis refers to predetermined times when the brain will kill off large amounts of capacity that has not been used. The two biggest apoptotic events are at age four and thirteen. As a result of these unavoidable deadlines, infants and children need to stimulated, model and exercise important identity features before those are deleted. For the child's brain this means extensive exposure to an adult with a well-trained relational brain and with whom they have a joyful attachment. Historically, this will be their mother.

Once the brain deletes unused cells, sensitivities and systems it is no longer true that the brain can produce its original genetic range of options. Critical exposure (mirroring) times are followed by intense trimming times. It is no coincidence that infancy and childhood each end when apoptosis starts. By now, whatever the infant or child needed to acquire had better be there or the chances that it will develop correctly are gone.

The brain develops strengths through apoptosis. A brain can do many things but it cannot be good at everything. By trimming back to what has been awakened, the brain can selectively strengthen the activated skills. A brain can desire an identity but after apoptosis the ability to change is limited.

Who we want to be is not simply passive or imposed by others. A boy who dislikes the men or women in his life can actively model his identity and sexual preferences to avoid what he dislikes. A girl who does not like how girls and women are treated can actively seek alternatives. Adults, friends and culture are also factors in developing preferences. These preferences develop strongly during infancy.

Early identification and activation of identity is needed before apoptosis starts. Without activation of identity characteristics before apoptosis, many characteristics will not be left behind to strengthen after apoptosis. The brain kills off the weak elements. Parents who are afraid their child will miss out on all the possible options may doom the child to inadequate functioning in many options.

What babies need are strong relational skills for building joy and avoiding enemy mode. Sometimes parents, communities and cultures lack important relational abilities thus leaving the same essential elements un-activated in their children's brains. My sense of ME can be shaped by people who cannot see in me what God sees. I will then fail to see in others everything that God sees in them. Without seeing others through the eyes of heaven my brain goes into enemy mode too easily and simply wants to win. We need brains that want to see in one another what God sees.

As a baby approaches four years of age (the first major apoptosis) an inadequately activated identity will leave some deformities in brain development. The ancient Hebrew word for deformities is translated "iniquities" in the English Bible. Common examples of biblical iniquities are being blind, deaf, paralyzed or mute. Each of those iniquities involves an obvious failure of some part of the nervous system. Jesus frequently healed these iniquities and pointed out that forgiving sin was easier that healing iniquities.[1]

Many people in Jesus' time (and even now) moralize about iniquities/deformities[2] wondering if the deformity was the result of the person's sin or maybe the sin of their parents. While sin, such as sexual abuse by family members, can cause iniquities, most deformities have many causes outside of anyone's control. Moralizing about iniquities is pointless and hurtful.

Learning about maturity always exposes iniquities in our maturity. We may, with considerable practice and effort, learn to manage deficits and even recover some capacities. We mistakenly think that we can will our way out of the deformities in our brain development. Such is not the case. What we need is more than willpower. We need a godly family and community to be tender with our weakness and still see our value. We still need mothering as we mature or remediate missing maturity as much as possible.

PREPARING FOR WEANING

When an infant has a close bond with his mother, he or she can depend on mom to appear and help him every time something bad happens. From this a baby learns that bad things precede comfort. He is not alone. He need not fear bad events or feelings. Confidence, hope and faith are built on this simple foundation.

---

[1] Matthew 5:9
[2] John 9:2

Consider the confidence of those who know in their gut (prefrontal cortex actually) that something bad is the precursor of something good. Such people are not easily swayed from their path by adversity or pain. The security of our bond with our mother gives us a strong rope with which to scale the highest peaks of adventure.

The stronger the love-bond between mother and child, the more securely he will climb. The stronger his bond with mother, the greater his capacity to seize life. Knowing he will not be pulled away from his mother's love, he can hold on to wild things and risk what other boys, girls, men and women would think impossible. He or she senses his capacity to stay on course even with some pain, upset and suffering.

NEVER step on a rope. Experienced climbers will tell you that stepping on a rope leaves little bits of sand that grind away the rope as you climb. Then, when you most need it, and tensions are the greatest, the rope will break. Children must learn to treat their bonds with their mothers carefully. Older children and family members teach younger ones to honor their bond with their mother and keep it free from fear, contempt or neglect. Mothers must also learn not to step on a rope. Mothers who confess their faults thereby teach their children to forgive and keep their bonds strong. If you never step on a good rope, your climb will be long and secure.

With a strong love-bond to mother, children can risk involvement without trying to control others, because even if they are hurt they know that hurt will soon be followed by closeness, comfort and healing. The child knows there is always a trail back to Joy Camp. The less they need to control others, the larger a child's world can become. More importantly, as adults they will not fear their partners or children. The needs and feelings of others will not feel like manipulations or control.

Mother is a preview and transfer point to God's love. Mother must extend her baby's bonds to God and others early in life. A mother's attachments prebuild children's relational world. Mother's secure attachments to God and others form bridges. The love-bonded baby builds on these bridges to become a life-giving adult, but we are getting ahead of ourselves, first our baby must become a child.

THE CHILD WITH INFANT MATURITY

Instead of preparing for the goals that come with each new stage of life, the disconnected baby in the child stage will continue to seek connection. They will want attention and resent it when others get any.

They will fail to meet their own needs and demand that others take care of them. You must make me feel loved! They will stay infants as they get older. Instead of seeking new goals they will keep checking to see if they have connections.

When bonds are based on fears, there is no way that weaning or any other stage of growth can go right. Babies raised on fear will not know there own needs and feelings clearly. If their mother's fears were fairly realistic, then they will cope fairly well with life; if her fears were exotic and irrational they will have little chance of discovering who they really are.

Bonds based on fear don't work well. These bonds can be broken by any fear greater than the fear that formed the original bonds. Stronger fears are usually produced by dangerous, abusive and predatory people who then become "attractive" to fear-bonded children and adults. This makes for poor relationship choices.

A true love-bond is characterized by joy, appreciation, encouragement, independence, creativity, flexibility, rest and the ability to risk. A fear-bond is built through control, anger, threats, shame, rigidity, rejection or clinging. As with most of life, nothing is perfect. There are few perfect bonds of love or fear. In these mixed bonds, fear stretches love as though it were a rubber band, if the fear proves too strong, the love snaps and fear takes over. When the fear becomes intense enough, the compromised control center comes apart. A weak love-bond will easily be broken by strong fear. Strong love will withstand great fear before giving way. These mixed bonds snap at odd moments and are tremendously confusing to children. They are also discouraging to fearful parents who want to love their children.

A mother whose own security is not strongly anchored in attachment love will quickly be overcome by fear. She desynchronizes inside and becomes confusing outside. Her frightened basic evaluation center (at level two) seizes control of her poorly developed mind. The frightened or angry mother will snap from love to fear as her sense of being threatened grows.

Karin loved her children. She hugged them, fed them, played with them, shared them with her adoring husband. She appeared to be a perfect mommy while Justin was a baby. But Karin had a flaw, a rather deep fear of rejection, which she pushed aside. True, she loved her husband and children and they loved her. When everyone was loving or even sad, she was the mom of moms. But, every once in a while Karin would "lose it" with her son Justin. She was always very sorry for it afterwards, but she just couldn't take it when he refused to do what she told him and ignored her. She would respond by yelling at him and even shook him a couple of times. But that scared her so she stopped.

Justin's unresponsiveness awakened in Karin a fear she always carried that her father's unresponsiveness meant he did not love her. This fear led her to try and scare a response out of Justin. Reliance on fear at formative moments with her son developed from the strong fear she always carried toward her father. If Justin ignored her, it reactivated Karin's feelings of being ignored by her father. In those moments, she produced in Justin the same fear that she experienced toward her father. Deep inside, Karin really believed it was fear that most profoundly connected parents with their children. The power of fear was reflected in how she acted.

During the childhood stage, a child with weak bonds will not be equipped or prepared to reach new goals. Unlike other four-year-olds who are eager to explore their father's world, take care of themselves, and make friends, the weakly bonded child is concerned about being forgotten or left out. During childhood this can best be seen in the way a child forms friends. Securely attached children are usually invited to play by others and allow other children to join in their play. Poorly bonded children are insecure and beg to join with other children. Insecurely bonded children are often rejected and play alone. When they do succeed in playing with others, weakly bonded children are frequently displaced or they reject any additional playmates who want to join. Billy was this way. When he had a friend his most common words to others were, "You can't play with us."

MOTHER AND HER WEANED CHILD

Let us return to our observations of a mature mother as the baby becomes a child. With Mother's excellent help, babies come to find out that they can need, feel, ask and receive. What a wonderful world this has turned out to be, a world where they can take initiative without having to feel guilt for trying. As they learn to ask more clearly, infants prepare for weaning when they must make a first solo stand in the world. Successful passage from infant to child requires a solid bond between a baby and mother. By training them to express needs and feelings in appropriate words and actions by the time they are four, they are ready.

Weaning marks the time when the child is officially on his own. Weaning, in the sense I am using it, involves feeding, dressing, walking, speaking for himself, and other skills that allow a child to separate from mother and achieve a basic level of independence. Mother is no longer in charge of guessing what the child wants. The child must now ask. Not asking brings with it not receiving, for Mother no longer guesses what is on a child's mind. Sure, children can solicit help, but even that is now largely up to them. With Mother's help, they have learned to put words to needs and feelings so that others can know them without mind reading. This is the first major achievement of childhood.

The well-bonded mother has her hands full with the weaned child at first. It is not easy to build confidence. Each child reacts differently when weaned as a child might when learning to skate or ride a bicycle. Some just take off while others very carefully test each step. But whether it is through encouraging or trying to keep up, Mother helps the weaned child become successful at this new stage of independence. She answers a million questions a day.

After a successful start, mother will steadily demand more from the child. He needs to ask correctly, at the right time, and to the right person. Soon he will be busy learning about his rapidly expanding world. As his perceptions allow more complexity, his requests become more complex. Before long he must begin to calculate time into his requests. This equips him to appreciate his part of history when he becomes an adult. To do so he must figure out ahead of time when he will be hungry and how much he will want to eat before he packs his lunch. Mother helps greatly by teaching the child how to manage time, such as getting his or her boots and coat on *before* the school bus arrives.

On the other hand, a child likes his mother because she keeps the world "soft" when each day it becomes increasingly "hard." Mother continues to be a stable source of warmth and care leaving him free to focus his attention on his world. He is free to try hard things because he trusts his mother's firm support, comfort, and acceptance. His mother helps him stay in the range of manageable mistakes by tracking his development. Since he can count on a soft landing if he falls, the child can practice climbing enthusiastically. Falls are learning experiences that make him or her a better climber.

A mother's special gifts of knowing children, which previously helped her know his diapers were wet, now help him know that he is interesting. Mother helps him remember early lessons about his value. She reminds him he has worth just because he is her child, not because of anything he can do. As a result, children continue sharing the world they are discovering with their mother.

As we have already seen, the unprepared child is in for trouble. Trying to be a child is very frustrating when he or she doesn't know how. He begins to think he is a failure. The child who does not know how to meet his needs by asking will quickly become angry. Unmet needs produce anger, and since no one likes an angry child, the frustration soon escalates as his anger triggers increasing rejection from others. The mocking phrase, "He just wants attention" is usually close behind, leaving him angrier and more disenfranchised than ever—a casualty of infancy and a badly trained control center.

Sometimes it is Mother who is not ready to let her baby grow up. If she tries to keep her child an infant, then they will have endless fights about wearing jackets, boots, or what to eat and when to rest. Sometimes, a mother keeps her child at infant maturity by continuing to be his or her voice. She tells the world how to understand her child's feelings, reactions, actions and needs. Particularly if the mother relates to her child through her own fears, she will have trouble allowing him to learn from his own mistakes. Not uncommonly this sort of mother makes a career of cleaning up the messes her children make. What a disaster that will be during adolescence when they start making a mess of their lives!

MOTHER OF ADULTS

The apoptotic period about age thirteen brings major changes to a child's brain that greatly weakens individual stability but prepares a young adult to form a group identity. Adults establish new points of reference for their identities and try out their power on each other.

Young adults need to know whether they should fear the new power they have discovered within themselves. They instinctively turn to their mothers to see if they are securely fastened for the arduous climb ahead. Does Mom still find them lovable, or is she afraid of their newfound intellect, body and skills? These special moments come in sudden spurts as young adults can go for long periods acting as though they could care less about Mom's opinions.

As young adults try to see their emerging selves, they return to look through mother's eyes. After screening out the things that Mom always says, they find consolation and hope in her stories about them. She reminds them that, to her eyes her child was interesting, lovable, and special even before they could do all the marvelous things they do now. She is a valuable keeper of their history even when it embarrasses them to think that they were once as helpless as Mom describes.

They share a little joke when Mom passes the sugar.

"Do you want some *oogoo*?"

"Oh, stop it Mom!" he grins. She alone could understand his language when he was a baby.

Young adults strain to understand what others are really thinking. This ability to sense what others need and feel helps bridge the gap to people whose worlds are different than their own. At the same time, being part of a working group identity takes adults back to their earliest days of life when Mother's attentiveness first broke through the borders of their existence. Their right brain "mother-core" is getting a workout synchronizing this newly developed group identity. Like mother, they now break though the borders of other people's worlds—now an attractive date, then an irritable boss, or again, a friend who has withdrawn and needs sympathy.

Men and women who want to deal fairly with others, have the first real chance to admire a mother's ability to know what others think. Like good mothers, adults now enter the lives of the people they meet and create joy by taking the time to know each other.

Mother-and-child relationships continue to be important throughout a lifetime. One simple reason is that each stage of maturity builds on the last. Each stage adds a whole new set of needs and tasks but does not remove any. Children must do all the infant tasks. Adults must do all the infant and child tasks. Elders must do all the infant, child, adult and parent tasks and there is a tendency to start ignoring the infant and child needs and tasks as we add more demands. Mothers have ways of reminding their children that they still need sleep, good food, play and clean underwear in case they are in an accident.

My wife Kitty went down to pick up our older son Jamie from college. It was the end of exam week for both of them, since Kitty had started back to college to learn sign language. As they settled in for the two-hour drive home, my son said, "It's good to have you to myself all the way home. There are some things I want to talk to you about." Kitty was delighted. They went on to talk about girls, dating, surpassing one's own parents and many other things.

Mother's encouragement means so much at these times. Her faith that he can cross this difficult terrain, even if he is far less skilled than she, brings the hope that he can touch other's worlds and be touched in return. The man who lacks this ability will find himself alone no matter how many parties he attends or how often he gets someone in bed.

The last major challenge of the adult son comes with his marriage. For his mother, marriage brings very important moments of receiving and releasing. Kitty prepared for this experience from almost the moment the boys were born. Each night we prayed for each son and their future wife, wherever that little girl might be in the world right then. We prayed for her safety, her health, and for her soul's welfare. You can imagine Kitty's eagerness to meet them some day. They were beloved strangers she had spiritually covered and waited almost twenty years to meet. Her mother's heart was prepared to receive a daughter-in-law and release her son.

I can hear her excited voice on the phone when Rami said he wanted to bring home a girl for us to meet. After she got off the phone she lay in bed talking excitedly about all the special things she had learned about the girl until well beyond my bedtime. How she liked someone who could love and enjoy her son.

When our boys got married Kitty cut off her apron strings and wrapped them around a book about mother-in-laws as a wedding present. She supported each young bride with a promise that there would be no fight for loyalty or control between them. Mothers have a lot to give their adult sons.

HER CHILDREN AS PARENTS AND ELDERS

One of the things that impressed me the most about my dad was his relationship to his mother. Even as a busy missionary for over twenty-five years, my dad wrote to his mother every week. Every week she would write back. Almost all of her letters ended with, "Well, I see the mailman coming now, so I'd better get this in the mailbox." These words brought a picture to my dad's mind of the little house he had helped build on 422 Bauman Road with lilacs in front and his mother sitting by the window. In the countryside of Colombia, torn by hatred and civil war, amid constant threats, he was reminded that he was lovable and worth protecting. So it was that his mother reminded him of how God saw him, even though she did not know that was what she was doing.

God's interest in spiritual adoption for fully grown people gives us another hint of the importance of mothers and fathers for men who are old enough to be parents themselves. It is interesting that Jesus spiritually adopted his mother and Saint John the Beloved when they were both adults. (John 19:25-27) Later on we read that the Apostle Paul, who was definitely an adult, had been adopted by Rufus' mother who was like a mother to him. (Romans 16:13) This he found very precious. Perhaps the man who had learned to be content in any situation liked someone to worry if his soup was still hot and if his tunic needed a little mending. We are never so old that we lose the appreciation for someone with the ability to see us and love what they see.

Mothers are at their best when they can see their children's unique history through God's eyes. Mary kept all the things she knew about Jesus in her heart. Mothers keep memories of their children deep in their hearts and treasure them.

One young man got angry and beat up his fiancée, whereupon she promptly broke off the engagement. When the young man returned to his mother, he said, "I just can't believe I did that!" His mother wisely began at the beginning and reminded him that this was not the first female he had hit. From there she told him who he had been, even back to his childhood.

She was indeed a good mother, for she told him not only his history but also who he was beneath the violence—a scared boy who needed help he could not give himself. Their family had passed along poorly running and badly trained control centers for generations. Well past her own children's infancy she sought repairs for her own control center. Now she was able to pass along new patterns. Mom's healthy shame message to her son let him see the problem and who he could be now. Repairs are possible!

WHEN YOUR MOTHER HAS DIED

I had many conversations (as a counselor) with women whose mothers had died young. Upon reaching the age when their mothers died they felt lost. They had no model or map. It is hard to know the importance of a mental model until there isn't one. One may decide to be very different from Mom but without a model it is hard to feel solid.

There are two ways a mother can die. The most obvious death is physical. Once a mother has died physically we can only remember her words and actions and, it is important to do exactly that.

Proverbs 31 contains the sayings that King Lemuel learned from his mother. Included among them is training on how to rule and marry wisely. She helps him to see what he really needs among all the options open to a king. "The women who make eyes at kings are not good for you," she tells him in effect, "look for a capable woman." She shares with him her ability, as a mother, to sense what is really needed by telling Lemuel to speak up for those with no voice, the wretched, the embittered and the poor. The King did well to remember his mother's words about who he was and what he really needed.

Scripture still contains his mother's sayings for us to remember. Just as mothers are to remember their children's history, children are to remember their mothers and treasure them in their hearts. *Never step on a rope!*

There is another form of death which is far worse than physical and much more insidious. Mothers and fathers who die this way still walk around and may talk to their children. These relationships are like marriages that are dead but the paperwork continues in effect. These relationships are dead but the facade continues to stand, especially during holidays. Such a relationship is death-giving to the families.

MAKING REPAIRS

When mothers cannot see adult children through God's eyes, these adults need another mother. Spiritual mothers, while they hold less of our history, may well be gifted with more vision of who we are inside. Like the apostle Paul, who treasured his adopted mother, we should form spiritual families. If saints and apostles need spiritual mothers then all of us could benefit too. A mother reminds us of who we are and how we are connected to others.

A spiritual mother will have her own gaps in identity and maturity but probably not the same set that our birth mother had. In addition, if a mother has learned to see in others what God sees they can awaken be-like stuff that has never been seen or activated.

Families will always leave gaps in our maturity. We often carry these deficits (deformities of maturity) with us to our own great frustration and that of anyone close to us. We will need to fill in these gaps before we can consistently act maturely. Since the later stages of maturity all depend upon infant maturity, let us consider how we can do remedial work in our next chapter.

Chapter Ten
Old but Still an Infant or Child

You can tell someone is still an infant when…

- Everything is about him—at his pace, when he wants it, how he wants it.
- If others have a problem with her it gets turned around to be her problem with them.
- When you go to him for comfort you end up comforting him.
- You have to read her mind to know what she wants.
- He grunts instead of asking.
- If she is upset you can't reason with her.
- He can't say what he feels.
- She can't/won't take care of herself or her home.
- He doesn't know what he really needs.
- She consumes (food, drinks, toys, TV, sports, sex, buys stuff) to feel good.
- Communicating with him does not solve problems.
- Whenever there is a problem she lets you know you don't love her well enough.
- He can't control his emotions or impulses.

The classic example: An elderly man fell and broke his hip. His wife was in such a state about his fall that when the ambulance got there they took her to the hospital leaving the man with his broken hip to drive himself to emergency.

However, men in this country are more likely to be stuck in infant maturity than women. Traveling the country and speaking to many groups I have discovered that somewhere around three of four men are stuck in infant maturity. About an equal proportion of women are stuck in child maturity. Once again, men seem to need a bit more redemption than women. This combination of infant males and child females is so common we need to have a look.

THE ADULT WITH INFANT MATURITY

Trying to make men grow up has been a cottage industry in America. Families wish their husbands, fathers and sons would grow up. Wives of men with infant maturity are at a special disadvantage. Wives cannot make their husbands mature. Even the idea that one spouse can make the other grow up is a sign of child stage immaturity. The more wives attempt to make their husbands grow up the harder the infants resist. What follows is usually a long effort to communicate problems and cajole a change.

For decades we have been told that the solution to marital problems is better communication but bad communication is not the source of all marital problems. Immaturity causes relational problems all on its own. Infants do not take care of what needs to be done. Infants do not keep their word. Infants do what their feelings dictate at the moment. This is true even when the infant can't express or even denies the feelings. Life with infants is a constant manipulation of feelings to get results. If you make him feel good you get what you want more often. If you avoid upsetting him you get less of what you don't want. Words mean very little with infants.

The extent of immaturity is not improving. As we pointed out in the book *Joy Starts Here*,[1] there is a steady drop in relational skills among people raised by screens. The lack of relational skills leads directly to a drop in maturity for both males and females. Critical periods of brain development are being spent with machines instead of duplicating mother's brain. When apoptosis arrives, unused human system are weakened or deleted from the child's brain.

In some ways we could describe the dysfunctional family as one in which the members are trying to get the rest of the family (or a particular person) to become like an infant's mother for them. A father, for instance, might expect his wife, or even his children, to guess what he wants without his having to ask. A little grunt, a turn of the head, or a tug at his coffee cup means he wants more coffee; and "mother" whoever she is, must jump to meet her baby's needs. Those actions resemble the infant's cries, turning his head toward his mother's breast, or tugging on her blouse for his supper. If the immature father's needs are not met, then like a baby, he believes he has a grievance—proof that he was not loved in the way that every nursing baby requires. Many

[1] Wilder et al, Joy Starts Here, (Holland, MI, 2021).

women become resigned to the fact that their husband is a child who grew old but never grew up.

Before we develop contempt for immature individuals we must realize that not everyone makes it out of the infant stage. Some babies never develop an adequate foundation. They spend the rest of their unhappy lives looking for someone who will read their minds, know what they need, and do it for them without their having to ask. Often these unhappy souls mistake this kind of care for love. Worse yet, they feel unloved if others do not guess what they want without having to ask. "If I have to tell them or ask for something it doesn't count," they say. These sad people never made it to child maturity. They still want love the way a baby does.

Because weak or fear-based bonds lead to weak identities, "adults" with infant maturity have trouble with anything that upsets them, or anyone near them. Sometimes they don't care who they upset and other times it is the opposite extreme—they are afraid to upset anyone. It can be extremely debilitating to be afraid of upsetting people.

Bud was the nicest guy you ever met. One would think all his relationships would prosper but, Bud was always worried. He stayed too long because he was afraid of missing out or upsetting friends by leaving. Bud often arrived late at his next stop apologizing, "I'm sorry I'm late but..." Bud worried about people's opinion of him. He was pointedly indecisive. Bud was a nice guy with infant maturity.

Bud married an infant woman who became upset very easily. He actually married her because she got mad that he had not proposed to her. He wasted his days trying to keep her happy. Trying to keep her from getting upset cost him jobs, friends, sleep, health and time with his children. After a while many people became upset with him, but the harder he tried the worse it got. He was controlled by the most easily upset person he knew. Bud was beside himself with anxiety—a nice guy going nowhere.

ADDICTIONS – PARTICULARLY SEXUAL

All addicts have a failure completing their infant task of returning to joy. Addicts, particularly sex addicts, also have some unresolved attachment pain. This early failure sets up a catastrophic failure to reach adult maturity. All addicts are stuck at infant/child maturity. For this reason, we often consider infant and child needs together when talking about addictions. Rates of sexual addictions are rapidly becoming similar for both genders particularly when it comes to pornography.

An infant-adult with weak bonds will continue a desperate search for connection. It is this lack of a secure connection with a mother that produces frantic addicts. Without this crucial baby-mother bond, baby-child-adult will continue a sporadic, frantic search for connection with someone or something. The fear of being abandoned and rejected by people makes it safer to attach to a bottle or drugs instead. Addicts will fear their own needs. Some men and women may act tough. They will do anything for the love, yet never find love to be enough. The infant needs someone to be interested in who he or she is. Someone *has* to be interested. That special someone must "really be into me." This love obsession feels like it will help me become me! Without completing the infant maturity tasks the obsession simply continues.

A woman once told me, "You know, it is the easiest thing in the world to get a man, all you have to do is act interested in him. You can have your pick."

An actor candidly told me, "I just can't resist it when a woman is attracted to me. I have to have that love. I can't turn it down." As a result of his failure to turn down any woman's attention, he had lost several important women in his life and gotten herpes. He looks frantically for a strong love-bond to tell him he is good, valuable, and interesting. He is still trying to find a connection with a woman that will let him nurse contentedly and take in the loving gaze he has always needed. Without healing deep in his soul, he will never give up his frantic search.

The typical sexual fantasy of men can be reduced to this: he finds a woman or man who goes crazy over him and can't get enough of him. While there are many variations, this fantasy remains the prototype. By their teenage years, infant-men have usually sexualized their need for connection. They use orgasm to turn off the message from their nucleus accumbens that says they are going to die for lack of attachment. Men who are attracted to pornography, for example, should consider that they may lack a connection with someone who will tell them who they really are—someone who is eager to be with them. Such a man might think that his highest glory would come from having someone go nuts over him. He has a deep wound that needs to be healed before he regains control of his life. Sex will not heal that wound, for as nice as it might seem to have someone who is crazy about your body, it does not replace your mother.

Men who grew up without learning how to meet their own needs through asking and receiving will often react to breasts as though they were some extraordinary good thing. This has nothing to do with whether the baby was breast-fed or bottle-fed. Not uncommonly, such men have a fascination with breasts, particularly big ones.

Now, indeed, breasts are an extraordinary good thing if we consider the wonder of how a woman's body becomes a fountain of life, flowing with enough milk to sustain life and promote tremendous growth. That is amazing, but such is not the fascination of the man with infant needs. To him breasts are a good object beyond his reach—a treasure cruelly kept from him by the powerful creatures that have them. Breasts are objects to be desired, looked for, stared at in a ceaseless fantasy to have them all.

How to get access to breasts can be an obsession with some men. There is no shortage of lingerie and clothing manufacturers willing to exploit the man who does not know what he really needs. He will pay through the nose for the things that do not satisfy and wonder what is wrong with him.

Girl-women who do not make it out of infant maturity are also unprepared to meet their own needs by asking and receiving. These immature women also develop their own fascination for breasts. However, since they own a set, the girl-woman's preoccupation is different from the infant-man's. Girl-women wonder about the adequacy of their own good-stuff. Their sufficiency is usually measured by attractiveness and the current fashions. For the woman with infant needs, displaying and simultaneous hiding her breasts becomes an obsession. Endless shaping, padding, covering with lace, changing necklines, finding the right tightness of blouses, buying seductive bathing suits and sleepwear, all become part of this quest for the perfect display. Surgeons can add their modifications if clothing and padding do not suffice.

If, by some chance, an infant man and woman should meet, the resulting interaction gets physical rather quickly. Even if no touching happens between the two, the woman displays her attractions to a man who works to possess them in some way, either by seeing more, or getting closer—much as an unhappy weaned child would try to get to his mother's breasts. Meanwhile, the woman tries to keep the man's attentions while staying just out of reach, acting out her interpretation of her mother's distance after infancy.

This frantic search for connection can lie behind family dysfunctions and even religious addictions. People tied to "toxic faith" often try desperately to do anything they can for God's love and attention, as though we needed to do anything in order to receive God's love. They have shaped their religion to fit the thinking of an abandoned infant.

The prophet Isaiah once wrote, "Can a mother forget the baby at her breast and have no compassion on the child she has borne? Though she may forget, I will not forget you!" (Isaiah 49:15NIV). To replace the delight of a God who loves us like a mother nursing her child with unconnected sexual passion or religious fervor, is like eating charcoal briquettes instead of grilled steak. It is close, it is hot, but it does not satisfy.

SOME SOLUTIONS

You may have recognized some gaps in your infant maturity or perhaps that you are still in the infant stage. If growing up was so easy you would have done it by now. Not being a "how to fix your life at home with twine and chewing gum" book, we won't attempt here to spell out quick cure for infant maturity. We can give a few suggestions to help you get started. *Becoming Me* is the focus for this book. So let's consider the question of where to start. If you answer yes to these questions go to the next item.

1. Can I quiet myself and feel comfortable in my body?
2. Can I experience appreciation when I try?
3. Can I build joy with others?
4. Have I reset my normal to peace and joy? (chapter three)
5. Can I experience Godsight?
6. Can I create belonging for others?
7. Can I restore joy when someone feels upset? With:
    1. Sadness
    2. Fear
    3. Disgust
    4. Anger
    5. Shame
    6. Hopelessness
8. Do I experience grace? (I can feel special?)
9. Am I moving out of predator to protector by sharing the pain of others?

You now have a starting point from any "no" answers. We cannot learn these things out of thin air. You may need a trail guide. Look for people who are good at what you need to learn. Look for someone who is high joy. Having a guide who can coach us will reveal places where we need more joy.

Begin by building joy with your guide and any willing people in your life. After years of living with low levels of relational joy, low joy feels normal. Because joy is the one emotion that infants will seek on their own, building joy is central to helping infants mature. Joy is one of the few areas of maturity where partners and children can genuinely help. Joy smiles, pleasant voice tone and lots of eye contact build bonds between couples as well as with children. I suggest lots of practice with smiles. Children and grandchildren are good places to practice smiles. It is particularly necessary to end each day with joy otherwise stress hormones like cortisol erase the joy developed that day during the night.

For more help developing joy I suggest books like *Living From the Heart Jesus Gave You*[1] and *Joy Starts Here*,[2] *The Joy Switch*,[3] Chris Coursey and Marcus Warner have developed a whole series of Four Habits[4] books for joyful people, marriage and kids.

People who lack joy are easy to recognize as soon as one asks the question, "Does she (he) live in joy?" As soon as we talk about building joy with infant-adults we discover that the people around them are often upset with them and in no mood to build joy. What they need is help returning to joy.

Adult infants will have great trouble returning to joy from at least one of the major emotions. We are talking about anger, fear, sadness, disgust, shame, or hopelessness. Staying relational and regulated in the presence of a distressing feeling is what we mean by returning to joy. In other words, "Even though I am mad, scared, sad, hopeless, ashamed, or disgusted I'm still glad to be with you.

We know how people treat us and what they value when they feel joy. The well-trained control center in a well-synchronized brain will keep the same values and intentions no matter the feeling. This is hard to believe if you have only seen ignorant, immature and untrained brains at work.

---

[1] Friesen, Wilder, Bierling, Koepcke and Poole, Living From the Heart Jesus Gave You, (Shepherd's House, 2015).
[2] Wilder et al, Joy Starts Here, (Holland, MI, 2021).
[3] Coursey, The Joy Switch, (Chicago: Northfield, 2021).
[4] Warner & Coursey, 2019, 2021, 2023.

Returning to joy is an acquired skill as we saw in chapter two. Learning to stay relational requires synchronizing mental states with someone who already knows how to be relationally stable in that emotion. This means finding a more developed brain that is able to feel misery and still act the same as if it were feeling joy. THRIVE Training[1] in person or on line provides models, guides and coaches. THRIVE also helps us reset our normal to joy. Books like *Transforming Fellowship*[2] help whole communities improve their skill restoring joy.

I suggest making a list of the six emotions and mark the ones you avoid. Also mark the emotions in which you treat others differently. If you are guiding someone with infant maturity make a list for them. Finally, write next to each emotion anyone you know who is good at staying relational during that feeling. i.e. Uncle Virgil is just as kind when he is mad as when he is happy. Vicar Rainwater is just as warm when he feels hopeless as when things are going well.

A person with infant maturity learns by sharing a mutual state of consciousness with someone who knows what they are doing in that emotion. This training can be done by face-to-face story telling about times you each felt the feeling. If you want people to train you and "download" their control center into your brain you may want them to read this book first so they know what you are talking about.

CREATE BELONGING

Belonging is something that infants create around themselves. An embryo grows a placenta and attaches to the womb. Infants will create belonging for whoever is around them once the baby is born. The major impact of trauma and neglect (low joy) is that we stop creating belonging around ourselves. We begin "playing it safe." That is rather like avoiding drowning by giving up breathing. We can understand the reaction but it does not play out well. Therefore, to mature we must begin creating belonging for others once again. That is our normal activity as relational people of joy. Creating belonging is explored in Life Model Works resources and the work of Ed Khouri.[3] For now we will simply mention that we build belonging ourselves rather than waiting for someone to do it for us. *He who would have friends must be friendly* the proverb says.[4]

[1] ThriveToday.org
[2] Coursey, 2016.
[3] Khouri, Becoming a Face of Grace 2021, Beyond Becoming, 2022, The Weight of Leadership 2022.
[4] Proverbs 18:24 paraphrased.

Grace is another element of the infant stage. Grace is the ancient word meaning we are special to someone. We need to learn we are special without doing anything to earn our grace. Ed Khouri has written extensively on ways Christian communities can learn grace.

There are enemies of belonging. Narcissism is the cancerous version of grace. In the book *The Pandora Problem*,[1] I explore the solutions to narcissism.

Predatory behavior also destroys belonging. Because all infants are born predators and need to learn to become protectors we must take a bit of time to consider this essential transformation. Infant predators in grown bodies molest others. Sexual addictions and domestic abuse require strong community intervention to keep vulnerable people safe and joy growing. Infants in adult bodies can and will abuse others instead of returning to joy from anger for example. If these problems are already present you will need to stop the damage and risks before growing maturity.

A hesed (attachment love centered) community is needed to learn how to be protective once a person is over twelve years of age. When it is safe to work on becoming a protector you will find books like *Joy Starts Here*,[2] *Transforming Fellowship*[3] and *The Pandora Problem* can help a hesed (attached) community address these issues. Families can teach protectiveness to younger people.

Forget talking it out, being understood, each taking responsibility for half the problem or coming to an agreement with infants. Communicating is not the solution to relationship problems when one is dealing with infant maturity. Partners of infants are very much advised to read the book *How One of You Can Bring the Two of You Together* by Susan Page.[4] Page shows how anyone can put his or her maturity to work and improve a situation. She calls it "being the bigger person."

HELPING MEN WITH INFANT MATURITY

Usually a man at infant maturity has a hard time realizing that he needs to work on his immaturity so we will start our suggestions with ideas for family members. The good news is that if anyone can motivate a man to mature it is his children. Motivating someone is quite different from

[1] Wilder, The Pandora Problem, (Carmel: Deeper Walk Publishing, 2018).
[2] Wilder et al, Joy Starts Here, (Holland, MI, 2021).
[3] Coursey, Transforming Fellowship, 2016.
[4] Susan Page, How One of You Can Bring the Two of You Together, (New York: Broadway Books 1997).

guiding that same person through steps of maturity. Let me explain.

If you want to help someone you love who has infant maturity, work on your own maturity until you can let their upset be their problem. The upset that infant men feel when they don't get their way is necessary for them to change. Even their brains do not register the need to change until they are stuck in an upset feeling-that, of course, will be someone else's fault. Infant men have mastered techniques for getting others to relieve them of their pain. If his wife stops responding, his children step in. If his children stop taking care of him his mother steps in. If his mother dies, his nieces or other women he knows step in.

Can you spell codependency? Counselors will tell you that the hardest part of getting infant men to grow is getting their enablers to stop enabling long enough to let some real discomfort have its motivating ways. Of course, this has real risks for marriages, for many an infant man has simply moved on to find another wife to enable him when his first wife grew up.[1]

If infant-men are in a safe environment, many will acknowledge their immaturity and want to change. Men are much more likely to admit this need to a stranger than they are to their family. After all, strangers are not going to ask anything of them. Most infant-men are aware at some level that they have failed to provide what their partners needed.

Here is the paradox—adult-infants need to be in pain in order to change but infants avoid pain and slip away before they learn anything that would help them change. Infants will only look at their pain if they have someone with them to guide them through to new growth. Infant-men have to feel safe with their guide and since their wife is usually seen as the source of their pain she is not safe. Worse yet, she may ask something of him he can't give. She cannot be his guide. His children pose similar dilemmas. The guide must come from outside the immediate family.

Predatory behavior is a constant part of infant maturity. Predatory behavior takes personal advantage of weakness. Like all state-dependent learning, being a skillful predator will depend on practice, opportunity and luck. Some predatory behavior can be as harmless as borrowing something without asking. So, why are we talking about predatory behavior?

---

[1] If you are dating or married to someone on a third marriage, that person is likely an infant or an enabler of infant partners.

Some people become dangerous. People with established histories of breaking things, threatening others, sexual-acting-out, self-injury, intimidation, substance or human abuse are going to be very motivated to use those options again. When we stop enabling and allow someone to become upset, the chances of a predatory response get quite high. Guides, safeguards and involvement from outside the family become necessities. Find guides who know what they are doing.

Let us be clear that when we have gaps in our maturity skills we can drop into infant maturity and pop back out. This means that men or women who are usually not either infants or predatory can flip when they are under the influence of substances, stresses, attachment pain or fall into one of the "big six" emotions they cannot handle relationally. At these moments their brain goes into enemy mode and predatory responses emerge.

To calculate the amount of work it will take for an infant maturity man to reach child maturity, go through the list of infant tasks and needs at the beginning of chapter two. Check off the needs and tasks yet to be done. Now make a list of who you know that could provide the kind of care and training needed to meet those needs and guide those tasks.

If you are not a person who prays, this would be a good time to start because you need someone who will give life to this man when they have no real reason to do so except, perhaps, that they are full of life to give. Look, there is no way a wife or children can raise a man to maturity. His family of origin obviously left missing pieces so that leaves the community to provide some mature parents.

Finding a spiritual family for an infant man is essential for him to develop maturity. What is a spiritual family? Spiritual people will see a child of God in others who are not biologically related to them. Sometimes a sponsor and a twelve-step program will serve as spiritual family. This spiritual family has saved many people's lives but twelve-step programs are limited in developing maturity by the fact that most members are at child or infant maturity. People with earned parent or elder maturity do not get addicted. For that matter, people with adult maturity will not be addicts so the pool of people involved in twelve-step programs reduces the number of elders available. Hearing this really upsets people at infant maturity in twelve-step programs because they know their group saved their lives. I am not criticizing twelve-step groups, but recovery groups were designed to save lives and build sobriety not maturity. By the same token, people who stay sober in community generally grow in their maturity.

Here is an example of a spiritual family and how it might work. A small church, comprised largely of cowboys and rodeo riders, asked me to do a men's weekend. During that weekend we talked about the levels of maturity and all the men identified their own level. There were two elders, about three fathers, five adults and twenty boys and infants in that group of men. Remember that when I say infants we are talking about men in their 20s, 30s and even 60s. Each of the children/infants checked off a list of the needs and tasks they had yet to complete to become adults.

By the end of the weekend the elders, fathers and adults decided (on their own) to help the boys and infants mature. The group, under the direction of the elders, assigned men who were strong in those areas to guide the immature men through to adult maturity. One of the least mature men was Bob, the town drunk. The elders assigned three men to him. When I returned to that town three years later, Bob was a sober father of two with a happy wife. Three mature guides, each glowing with pride, pointed out to me how Bob had grown.

So, what had Bob grown? It was his identity, his ME, his fast-track emotional control system, his maturity, his ability to take care of himself so he could become an adult. Becoming an adult is what we do when we complete the infant and child stages of maturity. Let's take one more look at ME and what we have grown in our last chapter of this book.

Chapter Eleven
Me

Before crossing the meadow where the cows were grazing, I carefully scanned for any bulls. The cows would keep grazing but I knew from experience that bulls would likely accelerate my departure. My scout troupe was in the high Andes mountains on a mission to protect these cows from a jaguar who had been raiding them. Memories of jumping barbed wire to escape charging bulls flashed though my mind. My protective intentions would not be appreciated by any bulls.

Without warning I tipped over and began sliding down the mountain on my backpack. Nothing seemed to stop my slide. I could see the gray clouded sky above me and feel the wet grass moving below me. I flailed my arms and tried unsuccessfully to roll over. Visions of sliding through a fresh cow-pie filled my imagination.

After about a half minute I stopped sliding. What had just happened? I had never climbed this high in the mountains before and just discovered thin air. Who would have known that oxygen would be so scarce?

Since I had been last in line, no one had noticed my fall. I was left to gather my wits, gear and catch up with the other scouts. We would be camping at El Cielo. Our destination was hidden in the clouds an unknown distance above us.

At thirteen, all major working parts of my individual identity were supposed to be in place. I was no longer a child and was now determined to take care of myself. My sense of ME worked fairly well. Each of my fellow scouts also got himself to the campsite in the clouds. We all felt fairly confident that we could take care of everything. Tomorrow our group of young MEs would chase a jaguar together.

We all arrived cold and wet. Our immediate project was building a fire with wet wood. We sort of worked together but it was mostly every boy for himself. Working well together would be developed in our next stage of life.

A WORKING *ME* IS MARVELOUS

This book has covered key needs and tasks for infants and children. We have followed the trail that develops a basic working ME at the core of our individual identity. Most of these core skills involve regulating our emotions in relational ways. We have augmented our sense of who ME can become through the eyes of heaven. By the end of childhood that ME identity is operating satisfactorily in the presence of others. Our rough edges have been worn off through play with peers.

There are many more elements to a working identity besides these basics. ME include language skills, reasoning, social signaling, self awareness, skill with cultural patterns, showing deference (as I did with bulls) and compassion. ME prepares ahead of time and cleans up afterwards. ME rarely need reminders about what needs to be done. I create belonging around me. When I look at others I can see their uniqueness and value. I find humor and value in the things that make us different. When I need new skills I can find people to teach me. I know my world well enough to get around safely. I can be given some power and won't hurt myself or damage things and people around me. How much power is the question.

But a child is still a child. What still needs to be developed is not that obvious or important to children. While childhood as been a tour of possibilities, adult maturity will be a time of selecting options. Children only think briefly about developing mastery then lose interest if it means limiting their options. Their capacity to expand feels unlimited.

Children have not developed abstract reasoning sufficiently to evaluate constraints and produce a realistic plan. Thus children are not interested in finding worthy work they can stay with for fifty years. Neither do they look for a stable spot in community life where they become part of the community fabric. Everything seems possible. Personal restraint seems unnecessary. Why turn down power that I might not be able to handle?

As we sat around the campfire that night at El Cielo trying to get warm, Medardo picked up the shotgun we kept close in case the jaguar found us first. Medardo had never touched a gun so he picked it up eagerly and waved it around at the other scouts. As he lowered the barrel toward the fire pit he pulled the trigger. Embers flew everywhere as the explosion rocked the night air. The boy he had last pointed the shotgun toward began screaming, "You almost killed me!" Everyone else was knocking embers off their clothes. Medardo stumbled backwards into the dark dropping the shotgun as he went. Between the power of the blast, the power of the cold and the power of the jaguar, no one slept peacefully that night.

Quieting ourselves in the presence of others is an important childhood accomplishment. Other indicators that we have completed childhood include: good emotional control, doing hard things that will satisfy us later even though we don't feel like doing them right now. We can push ourselves when needed and care for our bodies by staying active and by resting. We work as well as play.

By late childhood, children need a mental model for how life works that is reasonably accurate. Life has patterns with major rhythms: birth and death, excitement and sadness, eating and being hungry. We are active in the day and sleep at night. Activities match the weather and the seasons. We feel sick and get well. Holidays and celebrations alternate with work.

While healthy children know about sexual energy it isn't from experience. Their motivation to find a life partner is limited and children often deny having any interest at all. But biology is about to change all that in preparation for developing *US* – a group identity that will mean more than ME.

BLOOMING AND PRUNING

While a child's brain is blooming with possibilities, every brain specializes by pruning – a reduction of options in return for speed and sustainability. Fast operations use less energy and are more accurate. Biological childhood ends about age thirteen with a major trimming of options.

The brain has a variety of ways to "clean house" but the net effect comes down to removing whatever we are not using. Most of us have had to move our home to a new location and eliminate whatever we were not going to need. We kept things we use a lot. Things we never used got culled.

Major apoptotic periods occur between infant and child stages (age four) and between child and adult stages (about age thirteen). During an apoptotic (brain trimming) period, the brain remodels itself. Brain circuits that have not had much use are removed. The brain systems a child will need later must already be in use through "play" in order to retain them.

Keeping all our options open means failing to become good at any of them. We can play piano, football, soccer, gymnastics, ballet, and swim while we study medicine, electronics, computer security, cooking, sales, crime scene investigation and astronomy but we will not master any of them. Play keeps lots of options open.

Specialization lies ahead. Specialization is on a biological timer. Specialization prunes options. Specialization means less diversity. Mastery and sustainable performance require adapting to rapidly changing conditions through specialization. But, and this is a big one, whatever systems the adult brain wants to specialize must survive the apoptosis leading to adult life.

A working heterosexual identity is one type of specialization. Maintaining a joyful marriage for a lifetime is even more specialized. Engaging well with one person of the opposite gender means that the brain skills we need must be practiced prior to the apoptosis of puberty. The relational patterns used in marriage must run rapidly, reliably and without much conscious thought by the time a heterosexual person reaches puberty and that big pruning begins.

It is a matter of biological timing to learn what will be satisfying before the brain does its scheduled housecleaning. We do not request or control its timing. Before the brain prunes systems for specialization those behaviors and patterns we want to keep it must already have a decent amount of practice. For a stable and sustainable heterosexual to be left after the brain prunes out the weak and unused options means that heterosexual patterns must be decently exercised beforehand. While the trimming will take place in the brain, practicing patterns engage the entire male or female body.

Adult life takes off quickly. Partner selection must occur early enough to develop much of the *US* identity together. Attachment interactions must be stable and good for all parties. The pair-bond must enhance performance of the rest of life's demands. Both partners must experience increased resilience even when things go wrong. Speed, accuracy and ease with relational patterns between genders will not be achieved quickly if the needed brain systems have been pruned severely and skills are learned belatedly.

Knowing common gender patterns serves adults the way standard plays do in sports. These patterns are practiced repeatedly by every player. Learning a standard set of plays (group patterns) leads to successful group actions.

The cultures I observed in my youth placed a high value on gender relationship patterns that had produced a sustainable culture for generations. These patterns remained stable for three or more generations. All boys learned a stereotyped set of culturally recognized interactions. Boys who didn't were said to be "raised in a barn." These patterns were rigid, taught early, practiced repeatedly and inconsistently satisfying to the children learning them.

For example, boys would lift their hats slightly when approaching a woman. The woman would nod and avoid most eye contact unless she wanted to engage the boy. There were culturally recognized patterns, much like dance steps, for: flirting, courting, showing status, deference, self-control, establishing territory, displaying performance, demonstrating health, strength, motivation, self-grooming, loyalty as well as the intent to escalate or deescalate a situation.

Humans are not the only creatures with social patterns. People have long been able to read the behavioral signals that animals use for communication. Birds learn signaling songs. Cuttlefish change color patterns. All kinds of creatures have mating dances. The young "play" with these patterns to achieve their standing and participation in their community. Skill with signaling patterns is essential for mate selection.

Human social signaling patterns are no less elaborate but are increasingly difficult to identify. In the next part of this series titled *Growing US: becoming an adult* we will look at common patterns men should know. The patterns distinguish a protector from predator, a king from a tyrant, a hero from a villain and a good mate from a disaster waiting to happen. I notice Western cultures increasingly expect each child to develop their own playbook without a standard set of plays. There seems to be considerable resistance to teaching or practicing what would be called the *compulsory exercises* if we were thinking of gymnastics.

When it comes to learning any sort of compulsory exercises in social communication, grade schools have no curriculum. Schools are like huge farms with only one crop. Grade schools are a very restricted environment for social signaling practice. One adult controls the room and children somewhat comply. Genders are homogenized intentionally. Of course, in their own estimation, schools are champions of diversity as long as everyone thinks the same way about diversity.

Public schools have been at the center of an ideology fight for several generations. Winners of these conflicts consistently characterize "our people" as the good people. The problem comes from making all "our people" into the heroes and "those people" into villains. Whether the conflicts are over ideology, control, power, politics, education or economics the newest "winners" convert the loser's heroes to villains. Thus, what "our people" think and value changes as power shifts. New gods are in vogue when the "oppressed" gain enough votes to become the "oppressors."

But the eyes of heaven are not so fickle and do not back the winners. Godsight is needed to see how every culture has its protectors, predators, avatars and best selves. It is mere child maturity to choose one side over another. Any creator God would be the God of all people in creation and have at least adult maturity—enough to pursue the good of all people at the same time. We all should develop adult maturity.

A sustainable, monogamous, heterosexual identity is even harder to develop than in the recent past. Social, cultural, familial, medical and economic changes have accelerated greatly. Learning sexual identity patterns early enough to sustain them through the pruning at the end of childhood conflicts with keeping every option open. Without early preparation, the chances of developing a stable, lifelong, heterosexual marriage partnership that produces sustainable joy are greatly diminished.

APOPTOSIS AND HORMONES AHEAD

Preparing for the metamorphosis into adults, means racing a biological clock that will alter a child's brain. Not only does this mean that some careful skill specialization should be in place but also that the child should have a clear picture of the challenges and opportunities ahead. The communities I observed in my early life had long histories of teaching strict and fairly arbitrary gender roles long before puberty. These same communities were very poor at preparing children for the emotional instability of the impending passage into adult life.

The sudden surge of hormones that come with sexual development adds instability to everyone. These chemical irritants make it difficult to self-quiet and feel good. Children who reach the adolescent apoptotic period with poor self quieting skills will lose twice as much of their meager quieting system as children with strong skills. The apoptotic process simply removes whatever has not been important enough to develop prior to its arrival.

Basic relational skills, identity patterns, healthy interaction patterns and a satisfying sense of self should be well practiced before the onset of puberty and the severe apoptosis that begins the adult stage. No longer will ME have the same priority in brain development. In fact, my sense of ME will be trimmed and significantly destabilized in preparation for establishing *US*—my group identity.

The effect of trimming a well developed self is one of giving priority and speed to whatever I have found to be very helpful and satisfying during my infant and child years. While the brain does not eliminate new options, the ability to develop neglected or undiscovered aspects of my self is considerably slowed and limited after the massive brain trimming that accompanies the onset of adolescence.

Trimming an underdeveloped ME is disastrous. The resulting identity is unstable, unhappy, limited, anxious, uncertain and unsatisfied with itself. Instead of having more options open for myself, I have fewer working options and more difficulty developing experimental visions of who I might become.

WHY BECOME ADULTS?

Our look at what happens during childhood is over and we must turn our attention to the next stage in our metamorphosis. If all went well, the twelve-year-old child does a first-rate job of self-care within the family and community. The child has seen the world and learned to feed him or herself well from the best of the land. Any boy with this experience is already ahead of the average male in the USA. A huge transformation now awaits him—his passage into an adult.

In more traditional cultures a boy would need to demonstrate that he had developed what he needs to be a man. Some cultures would send him off alone to take care of himself, do something difficult, earn his name or endure something painful. Other cultures would expect participation in some demanding social gathering that marked the boys readiness to keep up with *US* through days and nights of dancing and group activities. These same practices are also employed with girls as they become adults.

Taking care of ME is still needed for adults. I simply need to be so quick about it that I don't have to think much to do a good job. Taking care of me simply does not take my attention away from taking care of you as well.

If taking care of you is damaging ME my identity has become fear-based. My fear-based child or infant maturity is trying to act like an adult. This codependent, pseudo-maturity pattern is often found in couples where the woman is at child maturity and the man at infant maturity.

Adults will have the minimal level of maturity needed to maintain enduring relationships that are neither dependent nor exploitative. Healthy adults are motivated by joy rather than fears and worries. Adults allow others to disagree. Adults pursue what matters, find the least harmful alternatives, encourage growth in others and find sustainable solutions for everyone's welfare.

THE TRAIL GOES ON

The day dawned cold, and rainy as heavy clouds swirled around us cutting visibility to less than fifty feet. After a cold night of little sleep, it fell to me to smoke the jaguar out of its lair – when we found it that is. The other lads would find the lair. None of us had the slightest idea where a jaguar might live. No cow had been killed the night before to leave a trail.

The cold, wet wind was a mixed blessing. It cut through everything we wore but sometimes let us see a few feet farther. Eventually the weather won and we returned to camp. Had it been a worthy adventure to show we were ready to become men or simply an exercise in survival? We came on this trip hoping to show we could survive and take care of ourselves. No one told us we had to, it simply seemed important and unavoidable to prove something – at least to ourselves. ME now takes care of myself with satisfying accuracy and speed.

The process of developing a working ME had been a long trail. My trail guides, however, could still do something I couldn't. They could take care of themselves and help me at the same time. Now that I could take care of one, could I learn to take care of two or three or maybe even more people at the same time? Could I be a satisfying contributor to others lives? Bringing satisfaction to myself and others at the same time would be the adult maturity prize.

Everyone I ever met arrived at the metamorphosis into adult at least somewhat unprepared. We all have our moments when we tip over or slide down the mountain. We need a community to help us develop missing bits of our maturity. We have already mentioned quite a few books that can help communities work together but is it all work or is it an adventure? In her book, *Ordinary Discipleship*, Jessie Cruikshank[1] uses her Harvard training in neuroeducation and wilderness adventures to create a hero's journey out of fear into a strong identity. Becoming adults is hard enough for everyone but for those who arrived a bit unprepared and slid downhill on their backs into a cowpie, Cruikshank turns recovery into a worthy adventure.

Let us reprise the big picture. What we have accumulated through infancy and childhood is a sturdy, skilled, tested, experienced and satisfying way to care for our body and identity. We can be ourselves in the presence of other people. We can engage in life with sustainable satisfaction and perform the standard social "dances" without much attention or effort. We recover well and quickly when things go wrong.

Most of life has been fun because it has been safe to make mistakes, learn and move forward. Our standard steady-state alternates smoothly between joy and peaceful quiet. We easily understand what others are thinking and feeling and can work together happily. Becoming ME has been a worthy challenge. I am up for challenges.

Now that I have ME, it is time to develop my *US*. In *Growing Us: becoming and adult* we will discover the needs and tasks that belong with the adult and parent stages of life. The trail goes higher!

---

[1] Jessie Cruickshank, Ordinary Discipleship: How God Wires Us for the Adventure of Transformation, (Colorado Springs, CO: NavPress, 2023).

Made in the USA
Middletown, DE
06 November 2024

64035721R00099